I Had Rather Die

Rape in the Civil War

Kim Murphy

Published by Coachlight Press

Published by Coachlight Press January 2014

Coachlight Press, LLC
P.O. Box 71
Batesville, Virginia 22924-0071
http://www.coachlightpress.com

Printed in the United States of America

Library of Congress Cataloging-in-Publication Data

Murphy, Kim.
    I had rather die : rape in the Civil War / Kim Murphy.
        pages cm
    Includes bibliographical references and index.
    ISBN 978-1-936785-16-2 (hardcover : alkaline paper) – ISBN 978-1-936785-15-5 (paperback)
    1. United States–History–Civil War, 1861-1865–Social aspects. 2. Rape–United States–History–19th century. 3. Women–Crimes against–United States–History–19th century. 4. United States–History–Civil War, 1861-1865–Women. 5. United States–History–Civil War, 1861-1865–Social aspects–Sources. I. Title.
    E468.9.M96 2014
    973.7–dc23

2013037412

To the memory of my friend Donna

Contents

Acknowledgments

Anyone who has written a book on a historical subject realizes the amount of research involved. Naively, I did not. Maybe that initial lack of knowledge was bliss. With an era as popular as the American Civil War, many period documents such as newspapers and diaries are available online. Penn State University has digitized Pennsylvania's Civil War-era newspapers, and the *Richmond Daily Dispatch* is online because of a grant from the Institute of Museum and Library Services, and a collaboration between the University of Richmond and Tufts University.

Cornell University library has digitized the 128 volumes of the *Official Records of the Union and Confederate Armies* and made them available to the general public. Vicky Betts, a librarian at the University of Texas at Tyler, has transcribed numerous Civil War newspapers with amazing accuracy. Many smaller sites also offer searchable archives and documentation. I am indebted to these individuals and organizations who made my early research seem easy.

At that stage, I had only intended to write an article. I never dreamed how deeply I would end up digging into various archives. When I finally realized that I was indeed writing a book, I began investigating civilian rape trials of the nineteenth century in order to see how they differed from military courts-martial during the war. Dr. Mary Block of Valdosta State University was most gracious with her time, explaining the proceedings of civilian trials to me. Our email conversations opened my eyes to a very different way of thinking regarding due process in the justice system.

A reference librarian and my friend, Sarah Johnson of Eastern Illinois University showed me where I could find many of the nineteenth-century civilian trials online. She also pointed me in the right direction when I needed guidance finding period newspapers that were not available online and how to go about getting copies of them via interlibrary loan.

For more than two years, I traveled back and forth to the National Archives in Washington, D.C., photographing military court-martial and service records. Many individuals tirelessly helped me locate the records and answered my numerous questions. With one exception, I know none of their names, so I wish to thank the entire staff. Everyone was incredible. The single archivist who I know by name is DeAnne Blanton. Not only did she aid me at the National Archives, she also answered my question about her own book, *They Fought Like Demons*, when I was attempting to locate an article about a female soldier.

I spent much less time at the Library of Congress in Washington, D.C., and the Special Collections at the University of Virginia, but the staff at both locations were wonderful to work with. Again, I wish I knew their names in order to thank them individually. I would also like to thank Leslie Rounds at the Dyer Library in Saco, Maine, for locating a soldier's diary entry, and Jill Jakeman, for scanning the entry and emailing it to me.

A special "thank you" goes to my editors, K.A. Corlett, Catherine Karp, and Sarah Grey, my cover designer Roberta Marley, and Faye Giles and my special friend Fataah Ewe for reading through the manuscript. And, of course, I wish to thank my family: my son, Bryan gave me a welcomed place of retreat before and after my many visits to the National Archives. My husband, Pat—not only encouraged me during my years researching a sensitive topic, he also accompanied me on a number of my research trips—and was often willing to help me gather information.

Ruins of Richmond, 1865

Introduction

"A Low-Rape War"

He took out his revolver and said, "God damn you, I will force
you to do it." He cocked his revolver. He said he would blow
me to pieces if I didn't let him do it.

SUSAN, A BLACK WOMAN, A SLAVE, and nine months pregnant at the time
of the assault, testified that Private Adolph Bork, 183rd Ohio, had
raped her. On the same day Bork raped Susan, he also shot and wounded
Private Ludwig Sweitzer. Testimony on both charges uncovered the fact
that Bork was drunk. While waiting for sentencing after his court-martial,
he escaped the guardhouse. Bork was sentenced to be shot with musketry.
The death penalty was mitigated to hard labor on fortifications or other
public works for five years.[1]

Few Civil War historians have mentioned the subject of rape, much
less studied the topic in any detail. In *The Life of Billy Yank,* Bell Irvin
Wiley stated that, of 267 Union soldiers executed, eighteen were executed
for rape, two for murder and rape, and one for rape and theft.[2] A few cases
involving rape and execution have been uncovered since Wiley wrote his
book in the 1950s, but his statistics are often cited by modern historians
to demonstrate that the Civil War was a "low-rape war."

In 1985, Joseph Glatthaar concentrated on General Sherman's March
to the Sea and through the Carolinas. In his discussion on rape, he included two cases that came to light during the march. One, he claimed,
was "instigated" by the woman herself when she used offensive language.
The other involved the rape of teenage Martha Clowell by Sergeant Arthur

McCarty of the 78th Ohio. The sergeant claimed he had paid Martha for sexual favors. This case will be reviewed in greater depth in a later chapter, but from these two cases, Glatthaar concluded that "criminal acts" against citizens were rare. He also noted that "nearly all the troops who wrote on the unjustified abuse... assumed that it occurred but also confessed that they had never seen such acts."[3]

George Rable cited both Wiley and Glatthaar and claimed, "Although physical attacks on civilians were surprisingly rare, some Federals handled females roughly." He continued his discussion, focusing on non-sexual brutality toward women before returning to women's fears of sexual assault. He stated, "Soldiers regularly intimidated mothers by threatening to rape their adolescent daughters, and even if they had no intentions, rumors and scattered reports of sexual assaults struck fear in many households." In the end, he concluded that rapes did occasionally occur, but the reports were "sketchy."[4]

Michael Fellman tackled the topic of rape during the war in more depth than preceding historians. His main focus of study was guerrilla activities in Missouri, but he included examples from other areas as well. He claimed that women who aided enemy soldiers "provoked" Union soldiers and guerrillas, but these men "did not shoot, violate, or beat" them. He cited one instance in which a woman by the name of Mary Hall witnessed the execution of her son at the hands of guerrillas, yet neither she nor her sixteen-year-old niece were raped.[5] Contrary to Fellman's statement, Mary Hall testified against a Confederate guerrilla at a military trial for attempting to rape her niece. In addition, the leader of the band was accused of raping another woman.[6] This case will be explored in greater depth in the final chapter of this book.

Fellman continued his discussion with examples of brutality against women by guerrillas and Union soldiers. He concluded that a code of honor prevented men from stepping over the line with their cruelty and raping the women. Women held the same values as men, he argued, and this value system offered a "certain general protection from men." However, this "moral framework" only applied to white women.

After a brief discussion in which he observed that black and Native American women were more frequently the targets of male hostility, Fellman concluded, "There are few direct reports, however, of actual rape." He proceeded to give one concrete example of three Confederate guerrillas accused of gang-raping a slave woman and stated, "James Johnson was sentenced to death, in part for his crime against a black woman."[7]

In reality, Johnson's death sentence was repealed, and he had not been charged with rape.[8] This case will also be covered in greater depth in the final chapter.

In *The Vacant Chair,* Reid Mitchell undertook a lengthy exploration on the topic of rape during the war. He cited Susan Brownmiller, a noted authority on the subject of rape, as a reference for the Civil War being a "low-rape" war.[9] Although Brownmiller did some investigative research on the topic, her discussion of Civil War soldiers was as a comparison to South Vietnamese soldiers. In the early stages of the war, Vietnamese soldiers had their wives nearby. Sex was also readily available through brothels. Brownmiller demonstrated that in the beginning of the war, with the presence of women in the camps, Vietnam had similarities to the brother-against-brother war in the U.S.; yet when the war dragged on and more soldiers were on the move, the sentiment of brotherhood faded and the incidence of rape increased. Due to a code of honor, men tended to refrain from raping their sisters or buddies' sisters because an "unknown woman is more easily stripped of her humanity."[10]

Mitchell asserted that Brownmiller's treatment of rape as a universal of war, which implied all soldiers from all time periods were equals, offended "the specific ideology of the northern soldier." He admitted that even though very few men were convicted of the crime, some rapes likely went unreported. He claimed it was difficult to "find much evidence for the rape of white women" and concluded that "one reason so few rapes were reported is that very few rapes occurred." He gave two examples of white women who had been raped, but reiterated that "few northern soldiers raped."

This was the case, he wrote, because "true manhood was characterized by sexual restraint, not sexual assertion; even mutually agreeable intercourse would have threatened masculine identity."[11] The 109,397 cases of gonorrhea and 73,382 cases of syphilis among U.S. white troops, however, suggest sexual restraint was somewhat lacking. In fact, some cities resorted to licensed prostitution in order to reduce the number of cases of sexually transmitted disease.[12]

Mitchell limited his scope to white women. "In both armies, black women seem to have been the victim of choice." He gave examples of rapes against black women and returned to a point made by Brownmiller: that rape in war might be an act against a woman's husband or father as much as the woman herself. Mitchell reasoned that because black women were considered property, more black women were raped than white women. He equated these assaults to symbolic rape against white women.

Once again, Mitchell reminded his audience that very few Northern soldiers engaged in rape due to "manly self-restraint." He ended his discussion with Glatthaar's observation that more black soldiers were executed for rape during the war than white soldiers. He suggested the reason might be white officers' prejudice, but Glatthaar cited examples of gang rapes committed by black soldiers. Mitchell suggested these rapes might have been "revenge rapes."[13]

Stephen Ash agreed that rape was rare, but "the fear of it continued to haunt women throughout the war." He cited updated execution statistics for the crime and claimed that Union soldiers who would never think of raping a woman "seemed to enjoy ravishing them psychologically." Such threats included "provocative and obscene language," while some soldiers exposed themselves. They also resorted to "rituals of degradation" when forcing women to cook for them.[14]

Catherine Clinton pointed out white women's status was based on their chastity. During the war, "Union justice appears to have been swift, merciless, and *not* color blind." About half of the men executed for rape were black; "race, rank, status, and other factors... affected outcomes." At the same time, she admitted almost no research had been done on the subject and concluded her discussion with examples of black women who had been raped.[15]

Other historians during the 1990s repeated and cited some of the preceding references. Ervin L. Jordan Jr. called rape "the silent subject of the Civil War," and Martha Hodes stated that "most wartime rapes, no matter who the victim, must have gone unreported."[16] In 2002, Mark Grimsley offered explanations for the mass rapes of American Indian women in the West versus the lack of rape of white women during the Civil War. Native women were raped because they were considered the "spoils of war," part of a systematic attempt to eradicate "Native Americans as a distinct people" as well as the "conquering army's celebration." On the other hand, Northern Civil War soldiers did not rape because of restraint. "Men raised to regard rape as wrong continued to regard it as wrong, even after three years of combat." In a footnote, Grimsley pointed out that black women suffered more frequent sexual abuse than white women and referred readers to Mitchell's discussion.[17]

Not until 2008 did any historian publicly question whether the Civil War was indeed a low-rape war. In two essays, E. Susan Barber and

Charles F. Ritter broke new ground on the subject and stated that approximately 450 sexual crime cases were heard in Union courts-martial. These crimes "occurred against white and black women and girls of all social classes." They used several rape cases to show that women from every class had been victims and explored how "the Union military managed to achieve some degree of sexual justice amid the chaos of war."[18]

Originally, I set out to write nothing more than an article on rape during the Civil War. Barber and Ritter had yet to publish their essays, and I had questioned historians' assumptions regarding the frequency of rape during the war. There seemed to be a general misunderstanding as to how people of the era regarded rape, not to mention that even today, rape is rarely reported.

According to the U.S. Department of Justice, more than two-thirds of rapes and sexual assaults go unreported during peacetime. In areas of the world where women have few rights, victims are even less likely to report the crime. Wartime statistics are more challenging to confirm because they are often used for propaganda purposes. In addition to the emotional anguish and blame associated with rape, victims during wartime fear for their family's lives as well as rejection from their partners and communities, making disclosure far less likely than during peacetime.

Susan Brownmiller has accused modern historians of the same sort of blindness shown by Northern abolitionists in dismissing sexual abuse under slavery as "illicit passion and lust."[19] The same can be said for some Civil War historians. Claims that the war was low-rape for white women while black women were the sexual targets of choice downplay the seriousness of the crime and demean the plight of minority women. Regardless of race, rape is not a crime of passion, but one of fear, power, and violence carried out in a sexual manner.

My research grew into a database of rape cases I uncovered from the National Archives in Washington, D.C., period newspapers, letters, diaries, and the *Official Records of the Union and Confederate Armies*. Commonly referred to as the *Official Records*, the 128 collected volumes contain the formal reports, orders, and correspondence of the two armies. Realizing that I had amassed more information than would neatly fit into an article, I decided to write a book.

No one has devoted a complete book to this topic—until now. More than once, I wanted to throw the manuscript in the trash. The women's stories that will follow are not only difficult to read, but heartbreaking in many instances. When I thought of giving up, their voices haunted me. *I*

Had Rather Die is their story, for their voices have been silenced for far too long.

In the first chapter, I will examine the background of rape laws in eighteenth- and nineteenth-century America. Without the necessary historical background, conclusions about the Civil War are meaningless. Terminology likewise must be placed in context. As with most topics of a sexual nature, euphemisms for rape, such as "insulted," "violated," "defiled," and "submitted," abounded. The most frequent term used by judges was "outraged." To confuse matters further, each state had its own specific laws, and by the mid-nineteenth century, degrees of rape were established. These often resulted in several lesser charges, such as assault with the intent to rape, indecent assault, seduction, fornication, and sodomy.[20]

Punishments in civilian courts reflected military court decisions. White men were typically given fines or prison sentences. Black men tended to receive more severe sentences such as hanging, castration, or lashes of the whip. As per English common law, rape was regarded as an accusation easily made by women and not easily disproved by men.

For a woman to make a charge of rape, she had to make an immediate disclosure, preferably to a father or husband who would help validate her charges; call for help; show evidence of being violently attacked; and been doing nothing questionable. If any circumstance raised doubts, then it was assumed that she had likely given her consent.[21] Legal decisions revolved around a woman's consent, which did not equate to how much force a man used, but the degree of the woman's resistance. Therefore, if a woman submitted due to threats of violence or because the man held a weapon, no rape had taken place—she had given her consent. Interestingly, such requirements for corroboration did not start to vanish from courtrooms until the 1970s.[22]

A woman who charged a man with rape had to openly admit to having unlawful sexual intercourse. The only sanctioned sexual activity was within the confines of marriage. In order for a man to be convicted of rape, a woman had to show resistance. A chaste woman, it was assumed, would defend herself to the death. Many courts dismissed women's testimonies because a respectable woman would be too ashamed to make such an admission in public. In addition, medical testimonies of the era frequently stated that nine out of ten rape accusations were fraudulent, making women appear vindictive.[23]

Before the early nineteenth century, a woman's past sexual history was regarded as irrelevant in a rape case. By the early nineteenth century, character evidence had begun to appear in rape trials, and by mid-century, it had become commonplace. Defendants could introduce testimony from the community vouching that a woman was unchaste; a woman who gave her consent to one man was regarded suspiciously with the implication that she would readily give her consent to another.[24]

The first section of Chapter Two deals with how the laws differed for non-white victims. Contrary to popular belief, it was not during the Civil War that a black woman first successfully accused a white man of rape in a court of law. However, it *was* during the Civil War that an enslaved woman was first successful in achieving a conviction of a white man. Prior to the war, the justice systems of both the North and the South did not regard the sexual assault of black women as rape. A few court rulings hinted that non-capital punishments were possible, but generally black women's voices went unheard.

The laws were equally disproportionate for men. Non-white men convicted of rape were handed the death sentence more frequently than white men—if the victim was white. In comparison, white men, if convicted, generally received a prison sentence. Some slaves were transported out of state or castrated if convicted of rape. Regardless of the races of the victim and the accused, women found it necessary to prove during rape trials that they had resisted their attackers' force and had not given their consent.

The second section of Chapter Two briefly covers the general topic of rape during wartime. Throughout history, rape has been regarded as an *incident* of war. Not until 1996 during the Bosnian war was it prosecuted as a *crime* of war. Few historians would argue against the premise that rape during wartime is common. Rape as a war tactic is not restricted to any particular army, country, or political system.[25] Throughout history, commanders' attitudes toward rape have varied from tolerance to strict punishment. Wartime rapes, however, are usually committed by small units and individuals.[26]

Because rape has generally been regarded as an incident of war, statistics were hard to come by until modern times. A number of American Indian tribes in the East were documented as having rarely raped white captives. Women in these tribes held important roles in their societies, often including leadership. According to anthropological studies, this type of example is consistent with cultures where rape is infrequent. In rape-prone cultures, women have low status and physical violence is tolerated. Sexual assaults tend to be allowed or overlooked.[27]

Chapter Three provides an overview of rape during the Civil War.

Many of the accounts in this section are "sketchy" reports from period newspapers, letters, and diaries. Emma Holmes, a South Carolinian,
wrote, "Wherever [Sherman's] army had camped, desolation, & defilement worse than death had followed."[28] Too often, these examples have
been dismissed as hearsay and propaganda. The *Official Records* are riddled with claims of rape in the same breath as plundering, arson, and
desertion—yet only rape, a crime deemed by nineteenth-century law to
be committed only against women, has been dismissed as rare.

In Chapter Four, I discuss black soldiers who received the death
penalty. Out of approximately 2.1 million U.S. soldiers, almost thirty are
documented to have been executed for rape or attempted rape during
the Civil War. More than half of those who received death sentences were
black. Black soldiers comprised only 10 percent of Union soldiers.[29] More
factors are at play in this situation than so-called "revenge rapes."

All cases in the chapter involve white women. Two cases are difficult
to analyze due to lack of documentation, but most of the men were involved in gang rape. Overall, these cases show that even though black
men tended to receive harsher sentences for rape, few were actually executed for a crime that was considered a capital offense.

Chapter Five examines the remaining twelve soldiers who were executed for rape. All twelve were white; many were foreign born. In civilian
cases, white men rarely received the death penalty. All of the victims
were white. Interestingly, only four soldiers were executed for the crime
of rape alone. Of two of these cases, the victims had male witnesses to
corroborate their testimonies, and the remaining two soldiers had a long
history of trouble-making.

On the surface, the actual numbers seem to reflect the view that
rape was indeed far from widespread, but there was an obvious prejudice against the soldiers involved. In reality, few men were executed for
a crime that was regarded as a capital offense and often believed to have
been dealt with harshly.

Chapters Six and Seven uncover more typical stories and explore what
sort of punishment convicted soldiers received, if any. Chapter Six covers
black women who were victims, and Chapter Seven, white women. My
aim in separating the two is not to perpetuate a racial bias, but to evaluate
whether the justice system treated women differently along racial lines.
The Civil War was a turning point in history for black women in that for
the first time their voices were beginning to be heard—but being heard
does not necessarily equate to justice.

Chapter Eight discusses gang rape. Only a few instances of gang rape appear to have been brought before general courts-martial. The men who were executed for gang rape will appear in prior chapters. Those who were not executed are covered in this chapter. Most of the records in this chapter come from diaries, letters, newspapers, and the *Official Records*. Gang rape is not uncommon during wartime, nor was it during the Civil War.

Finally in Chapter Nine, Confederate rapists are discussed specifically. Less evidence is available about the Confederate Army due to the fact that most of the records were lost or destroyed. Confederate rapists did exist. However, most wartime rapes are carried out against the enemy, and Confederates rarely ventured beyond their boundaries. Most of the existing Confederate records are from the areas where guerrilla tactics were common and from the few times Confederate soldiers had traveled north.

Throughout the book, I have resorted to the unconventional use of given names for the victims, rather than surnames. In Sharon Block's study of *Rape & Sexual Power in Early America*, she used personal names for both the victim and the accused. Her reason for doing so was to avoid subtle racism, since black men accused of rape during the colonial era were often identified solely by their given name, while white victims' surnames were used. During the Civil War, soldiers were referred to by their full names, ranks, and regiments, and the documentation mentioned race if the accused was black. Black women were frequently identified by their given names and race, whereas white women were usually addressed by their surnames. Like Block, I do not want to add to the racial imbalance by addressing the victims differently. In addition, rape is a very personal crime due to forced sexual contact; the use of given names better demonstrates the personal nature of the experience and allows the women to tell their stories as much as possible.

Historians who assert that Victorian mores somehow imposed gentle-manly restraint during wartime are ignoring the fact that rape is a crime of violence, not sexual desire. Wars in which prostitutes were easily accessible, show no relationship between sexual availability and the number of rapes carried out. During the Civil War, few on either side viewed sexual assaults on black women as a crime, and white women who dared make an admission of being raped were systematically ostracized. As in modern warfare, fear would have been a powerful incentive for rape survivors to remain silent.

But for women like Susan, who bravely came forward and relayed their stories in an attempt to seek justice, my sincerest wish is to make their voices heard. Perhaps future researchers and historians will treat the subject with the weight it deserves. The records exist and have largely been ignored due to romanticism about the era. This book aims to change that view.

Chapter One

"An Accusation Easily to Be Made"

Rape Laws in Early America

> It is true that rape is a most detestable crime, and therefore ought severely and impartially to be punished with death; but it must be remembered, that it is an accusation easily to be made and hard to be proved, and harder to be defended by the party accused, tho never so innocent.[1]

Sir Matthew Hale, *The History of the Pleas of the Crown* (1736)

MANY NINETEENTH-CENTURY RAPE LAWS centered around Sir Matthew Hale's declaration, which was first published fifty years after his death. Hale, an influential English judge during the seventeenth century, advised jurors that women made false accusations against men, and his warning became the basis of rape laws well into the twentieth century.

In Massachusetts, forty rapes and attempted rapes reached the high courts between 1698 and 1797. On the surface the number of cases appears to support the premise that rape was rare in Puritan society. As in present-day society, accurate statistics can never be established due to the fact that most cases never get reported, but investigation reveals some trends. In these forty cases, only one rape by an upper-class white man ever came to public attention; married women as well as girls under the age of ten had a better chance of bringing their cases to court, especially if the accused men were black or laborers.[2]

In Pennsylvania, during the same approximate time period (1691–1800), rape was a capital crime, but only when the victims were white females. Pennsylvania had fifty-seven rape cases and thirty-eight attempted rape charges. One in five of these cases involved children. As in Massachusetts, white women of a distinguished social standing were more likely to be taken seriously and have their cases received by the courts. Usually regarded as property, black women had little recourse until the abolition of slavery in 1780. Even after that date, few jurors were willing to sentence a white man for assaulting a black woman. Of the seven known cases where rapists received the death penalty, four or five of those convicted were black men.[3] Colonial rape laws centered around two considerations: how much force a man used and a woman's consent.[4] According to social norms, a proper woman guarded her chastity with her life. Therefore consensual and forced sexual intercourse merged. Social attitudes justified that a man could resort to force in order to receive a woman's consent. Juries were influenced by a woman's class, age, and reputation, as well as the status of the man she accused. Many men presumed women of lower classes could be bought for sexual favors.

A social double standard existed. Literature, diaries, and court rulings from the era portrayed women as desiring sex. However, women who accused men of raping them were considered untrustworthy, because pure women were expected to resist men to the fullest in order to maintain their virtue. Colonial stories in all forms of print, from newspapers to novels and plays, frequently depicted women who would rather die than "allow" themselves to be raped. Another commonly held belief was that modesty prevented women from admitting to being sexually assaulted.

Acknowledging that a rape had taken place was only part of a woman's battle. Support from a family patriarch was necessary for a rape charge to go to court. Women who had no husband or father to speak on their behalf hesitated to bring charges against rapists, due to an intimidating male-dominated court system.

Once in court, an accuser had to prove how much resistance she had used against the man's force. She was further questioned on how soon following the attack she had disclosed it to others. If she had significant bruising and had cried for help, she was more likely to be believed. Her answers determined whether she had fought sufficiently against the man and whether she had given her consent.

William Blackstone, an eighteenth-century legal scholar, defined rape by English common law as the "carnal knowledge of a woman forcibly and against her will," a crime considered punishable by death. Statutory rape was "the abominable wickedness of carnally knowing or abusing any woman child under the age of ten years." He further stated that Matthew Hale felt the age should be set at twelve years, but in reality the law only extended to girls under the age of ten. Colonial states remained divided in their age limitations.

Blackstone also wrote that common law dictated that "a male infant, under the age of fourteen years, is presumed ... incapable to commit a rape, and therefore ... cannot be found guilty of it." The law generally regarded prostitutes as incapable of being raped and did "not allow ... any punishment for violating the chastity of her, who hath indeed no chastity at all, or at least no regard to it." An exception existed if a prostitute had given up that way of life.

For a case to go to court, a witness had to be competent and credible. The law specified that to be credible a woman to be of "good fame; if she presently discovered the offence, and made search for the offender; if the party accused fled for it; these and the like are concurring circumstances, which give greater probability to her evidence." In contrast, a woman of "evil fame and stands unsupported by others; if she concealed the injury for any considerable time," may not have cried out during the attack or been in a place that would have made the attack a foregone conclusion; "these and the like circumstances carry a strong, but not conclusive, presumption that her testimony is false or feigned." In addition, children required competent witnesses to support their testimony.[5]

In early-nineteenth-century Virginia, the description of a man's force along with a woman's resistance appeared in court transcripts. "Force must be such as may reasonably be supposed adequate to overcome the physical resistance of the woman, taking into consideration the relative strength of the parties, and other circumstances of the case, such as making outcries and giving alarm."[6] Hale's caution is repeated in the lengthy document describing what rape did and did not consist of; if a woman only had minor bruises, it was generally disbelieved that she had resisted with all of her strength.

A white woman in colonial courts had a greater chance of getting a conviction if her attacker was black. After the Revolution, most men who were executed for rape were black.[7] Even in an attempted rape, a slave faced the threat of execution.[8] Castration was another form of punishment for black men; Virginia did not repeal its law until 1823 for slaves. In other states, castration laws were overturned later in the century, and as late as 1854, a Missouri slave was castrated for attempting to commit rape.[9] In many states black men represented two-thirds of defendants though they were a minority of the population. Southern courts had separate trial systems for black men, whether they were free men or slaves.[10]

Until the late eighteenth century, black women had little recourse. As slavery began to be abolished in the North, a few rape cases on behalf of black women made their way to the courts, but many whites resisted the change. In 1793, a defense attorney argued, "If Negroes be admitted to witnesses against white people. Rapes would be [charged] every day against white men by female Negroes."[11] The judges were divided two to three in favor of allowing Phillis Miller, a free black woman, to testify as a witness, paving the way for black women's voices to be heard. Even then, the defendant was accused of the lesser charge of assault and battery. Few juries and courts took black women's accusations against white men seriously.

Common-law cases from the colonial period paved the way for nineteenth-century rape laws.

Rape Laws in the Nineteenth Century

As in the eighteenth century, rape trials in the nineteenth century centered around the issue of consent. Most states established the age of consent at ten years. Kentucky, Virginia, Indiana, and Iowa differed by setting the age at twelve. Only Arkansas set the age at the "onset of menses."[12] Women who were insane or unconscious also could not give consent.

A boy of fourteen or younger was considered incapable of rape. In 1864, Sam, a slave, who was listed as somewhere between the ages of seven and fourteen in the court documents, was brought to trial for assaulting four-year-old Camilla Ann Brock with "an intent to forcibly and against her will, carnally to know her." An "emission of seed" was found on the victim, but the defendant was found not guilty because of "physical impotency" due to the fact that he was underage.[13]

Some states required proof of ejaculation for a case to be tried as rape.[14] In 1860 North Carolina, a fifteen-year-old boy threw Louisa E. Wheeler, approximately nine years old, to the ground. "He hurt her very much when he entered her person, and made her private parts bleed." Afterward, he took a switch and whipped her until she promised not to tell her mother. A day later, Doctor Pugh examined Louisa.[15] Her "private parts" were "torn and lacerated.... He was decidedly of opinion that the entry had been as far as possible in a child of her age." Because no ejaculate was discovered, the judgment granted the accused a new trial.[16]

As late as 1871, Ohio argued over whether ejaculation was necessary for rape to have been committed. William Blackburn had been convicted of raping Mary Donnelly. The state supreme court was asked to reverse the previous court's decision on the basis that there had been no proof of "emission as well as penetration." Blackburn was granted a new trial.[17]

By the middle part of the century, courts established degrees of rape, creating the lesser charges of assault with the intent to rape, indecent assault, defilement, seduction, fornication, and sodomy.[18] Rape was the only type of assault case that required the victim to defend herself. Defilement, seduction, fornication, and sodomy involved criminal sexual intercourse without the use of force.

In 1856, twelve-year-old Samantha Eustatia Hakes woke during the night. Charles Pollard, "who had got in bed with her ... was in the act of sexual intercourse with her." Samantha told Pollard to "go away," but he replied that "he would not hurt her." Because Samantha "made no outcry and made no resistance," the Iowa Supreme Court granted Pollard a new trial. "Forcible defilement" was determined to be a situation in which "the will is subdued to submission by menace or duress" but without the use of force.[19]

On the other hand, the charge of "seduction" was based on a woman who was "tempted, allured, and led astray from the path of virtue, through the influence of some means employed by the man, until she freely consents to the sexual connection." In an 1868 court case, a fifteen-year-old girl consented to sexual intercourse because the defendant had gotten into bed with her and choked her. On a second occasion:

> She yielded to him partly on account of his threats, and partly because the defendant hurt her. The ultimate consent ... might have been gained solely because the defendant hurt her, and through threats of further personal violence. And if this were so, then it is ... not seduction, but one of greater atrocity. But notwithstanding the defendant treated the girl roughly at first, and actually threatened to kill her, yet if she afterwards freely consented to the sexual intercourse, being enticed and persuaded to surrender her chastity by means employed by him, then the offense is seduction.[20]

The popular perception was that if no force had been used in committing the crime, then no rape had taken place.

Another case of seduction left one man dead, when C.B. Anderson discovered his wife in bed with another man, Major George Turner. Anderson shot and killed Turner, but Mrs. Anderson was said to have been around eighteen and "fond of dress." The moral of the story according to the *Richmond Daily Dispatch* was:

> This tragedy should teach married women the danger they run in attempting to dress beyond their means and to attract the admiration of men; it should teach all the danger of admitting to terms of intimacy men of whose history and principles they know nothing; it should teach officers and soldiers that seduction cannot escape punishment.[21]

In an unusual seduction case, James Mann was convicted to serve twenty years of hard labor for tempting Miss Hamilton, a "respectable young lady," under a "promise of marriage." His act had "consigned her to a life of disgrace or penitence."[22] The severity of the punishment suggests the woman was most likely the daughter of a wealthy, influential man, while Mann had belonged to a lower class.

Doctors were sometimes called in as expert witnesses at rape trials. False accusations were considered the standard, due to women's spitefulness or desire for revenge. Any rape accusations made against men over the age of sixty were immediately called into question. Common medical opinion held that a healthy, adult woman could *not* be raped.

Dr. Theodoric Beck, an early nineteenth-century physician, quoted Metzger's *Principles of Legal Medicine*: "For a woman always possesses sufficient power, by drawing back her limbs, and by the force of her hands, to prevent insertion of the penis." Only three exceptions existed to Metzger's rule: "where narcotics have been administered—where many are engaged against the female—and where a strong man attacks one who is not arrived to the age of puberty." Beck added his own exceptions: "fear or terror may operate on a helpless female—she may resist for a long time, and then faint from fatigue, or the dread of instant murder may lead to the abandonment of active resistance."[23]

An 1861 Iowa Supreme Court judge cited Beck's examples. Although she had been unwell, thirty-four-year-old Elizabeth Linney was considered to be of ordinary strength in mind and body, but she had no bruises. Even though the judge felt there was sufficient evidence that the defendant had made an assault with the intent to commit rape, "there was such an absence of force by the defendant, and so little evidence of the unwillingness of the prosecutrix."[24] On that basis, the court reversed the previous court's judgment and the defendant was awarded a new trial.[25]

Another legal medical text described how a woman's bruises had to be carefully inspected, as they might have been "self-inflicted, with the view to sustain her testimony. . . . Notwithstanding the violence, the conduct of the female may have been such as to imply consent on her part," or "she may have consented after the infliction of violence."[26]

In an 1860 Vermont court case, servant girl Orilla Vincent testified, "He took hold of me and pushed me against the flour barrel. I told him to let me go, he hurt me against the barrel. He then pushed me on the floor and forced me." She continued, "John came into the pantry before he got through. He staid there longer, an hour and a quarter in all. He lay on me just as long as he wanted to. He lay on me till I heard somebody coming."

The woman Orilla worked for, Mrs. John Rockwell, also took the stand. "She made no complaint until I spoke to her and asked her what was the matter; she then complained of his abusing her. I saw some prints of nails on her arms, and some spots rather black and blue." Two doctors testified that in spite of the bruising, rape was "practically impossible" under the circumstances, "unless she had consented." John Hartigan was found guilty of the lesser charge, assault with the intent to commit rape—not rape.[27]

For illegal sexual intercourse to have been considered rape, not only was it necessary for the man to use force, but a woman had to resist to the utmost. In a New York case, Judge Bronson offered his opinion:

> In such cases, although the woman never said "yes," nay more, although she constantly said "no," and kept up a decent show of resistance to the last, it may still be that she more than half consented to the ravishment. Her negative may have been so irresolute and undecided, and she may have made such a feeble fight as was calculated to encourage, rather than repel the attack. And yet a sense of shame, arising either from an apprehension of the consequences which may follow the illicit connection, or from the fact that the matter has already become known to others, may stimulate the woman to call that a rape, which was in truth a sin of much less odious character.

Specifically, the judge believed that victim Huldah Hulse had lied about a rape to keep from admitting to not have resisted to the utmost, thereby making her "whole story... a tissue of falsehood from beginning to end."[28]

Judge Bronson displayed an attitude common to judges and juries during the nineteenth century. Popular conceptions of consensual sex often portrayed men as the aggressors and women the resistors. Men created consent where none had existed. In Maine, a ten-year-old girl was beaten and raped. A jury found the defendant guilty, but on appeal, the chief justice argued whether "by force" equaled "violently." Judge Tenney quoted *Webster* dictionary, pointing out that "to force" was an active verb and equated to "to ravish, to violate by force," where "violently" was an adverb with a more general meaning. In the end, even though the defendant had assaulted Sarah Jane Lowell "violently and against her will," Judge Tenney concluded that "violently" was not the same as "by force." The defendant was let go.[29]

In a California case, a man raped a thirteen-year-old girl and threatened to kill her; she did not cry out during the attack. The defendant introduced evidence of the girl's "lewdness" with other men. Therefore, "there would have been less probability of resistance upon the part of one already in debauched mind and body." Chief Justice Murray stated:

> The case before us is supported alone by the evidence of the prosecutrix, a young, ignorant girl... and is so improbable of itself as to warrant us in the belief that the verdict was more the result of prejudice or popular excitement, than the calm and dispassionate conclusion upon the facts by twelve men sworn to discharge their duty faithfully.

The defendant was granted a new trial.[30]

A landmark case in 1838 led the way for not only how much resistance a woman had to use against the man's force, but the use of character evidence as well. Before this time, "character" had been determined by English common law to mean general character.[31] In the courts, character evidence was limited to a person's overall reputation, not individual acts. Women who were commonly regarded as prostitutes were looked upon with suspicion, but their prior sexual acts were inadmissible in court unless the acts had taken place with the defendant.

Judge Cowen of New York went a step further than traditional common law, after pointing out that the defendant "was not only a husband but a clergyman; and it may be assumed that he would avoid all improper appearances." Based on the opinion that the victim, Mercy Foster, might have had sexual intercourse with other men besides the defendant, he stated:

> A mixed case will not do; the connection must be absolutely against her will. Are we to be told that previous prostitution shall not make one among those circumstances which raise a doubt of assent? That the triers should be advised to make no distinction in their minds between the virgin and tenant of the stew? Between one who would prefer death to pollution, and another who incited by lust and lucre, daily offers her person to the indiscriminate embraces of the other sex?

In Judge Cowen's lengthy statement on the subject, he agreed that any woman, including a prostitute, deserved equal treatment under the law if she had been raped. But a prostitute required stronger evidence in court. He also went on to say that "an isolated instance of criminal connection [meaning any sexual intercourse without the benefit of marriage]" made one a "common prostitute." He doubted the defendant had been "guilty even of simple assault and battery."[32] According to Judge Cowen, women were responsible for their victimization, and a chaste woman would choose to die over being raped. Not all judges agreed with Cowen that a woman's past sex life was relevant, but such charges became a growing trend.

In 1847 Georgia, Cynthia Emeline Davis was assaulted, and the defendant was found guilty of assault with intent to commit rape. However, "on the part of the prisoner it was proven that she was a woman of ill fame, the defendant appealed the case, and it went to the state's supreme court." Judge Nisbet claimed, "Men are ... put in the power of abandoned and vindictive women." He quoted Dr. Blackstone, that women of "evil fame" usually gave false testimony, and continued: "Now, who is more likely to consent to the approaches of a man, the unsullied virgin and the revered, loved and virtuous mother of a family, or the lewd and loose prostitute, whose arms are opened to the embraces of every coarse brute who has money enough to pay for the privilege?"

The defendant's conviction was reversed based on the conclusion that a prostitute could not possibly tell the truth. Even though she had been beaten, as a "loose" woman, Cynthia would have "consented" to the man's advances.[33]

Men who were convicted of rape were often released early. In 1852 Virginia, serial rapist Bartholomew Maloney was sent to prison for forty years "as principal and aider and abettor in the commission of a rape. He was convicted in 10 cases, 4 years each." He was released in 1861.[34]

As in the previous century, those who were the most successful in getting rape convictions in the courts were upper-class white women. Poor women were extremely vulnerable to being labeled prostitutes. The double standard informed women of all classes that they should guard their chastity with their lives in order to maintain their purity. Women were considered passive creatures who sought protection from men. Such a weakness made women defenseless without men, yet in regard to sexual abuse, they were expected to be more aggressive and stronger than men.

In cases where raped women had male protectors, the law viewed the assaults as a property crime. Hence, violated women became damaged goods. White men accused of rape were typically given fines or prison sentences. Black men often received more severe punishment. Yet, few men found guilty for the crime received harsh convictions. These views and punishments were consistent with military court decisions and subsequently represented the foundation for rulings during the Civil War.

The laws of the early nineteenth century effectively reduced women's bodies to possessions of men; Hale's warning "of an accusation easily to be made" echoed throughout the courtrooms and well into modern times.

Chapter Two

"Fate Worse than Death"

Rape Laws for Nonwhites

BLACK WOMEN IN THE EARLY TO MID-NINETEENTH CENTURY had little re-course when they were raped. Few courts took their accusations against white men seriously. However, some women were successful in getting their cases to court. In 1818, Ellen Carsen, an indentured servant in New York, accused Charles Carpenter, a white man, of rape. When Ellen's master and mistress went out for the evening, Carpenter entered the house unannounced. Ellen felt threatened and fled, but he ran after her, dragged her into the alley, and raped her. A neighbor heard her cries and caught Carpenter leaving the scene.

The prosecution took exception to the fact that Ellen was an inden-tured servant and attempted to have her testimony disqualified. The court disagreed. Carpenter had attempted to bribe Ellen with money in ex-change for sex and she had refused. A neighbor testified that Ellen had been in tears "and her clothes torn to pieces." Two doctors swore to viewing her bloody clothes and verified that she suffered symptoms "of violation." Another doctor testified on the behalf of Carpenter's defense that he was affected by syphilis at the time and "in a state of great debil-ity." A ship captain also stated that Carpenter was of good character.

In spite of several witnesses who had heard Ellen's cries and saw her bloody clothes, the mayor gave a speech to the jury on how the crime of rape "stains the character of man. It was a crime, too, most unfortunately, which by our rules of evidence, the most malignant and depraved of the

female sex, may, by her single oath, fasten upon the most worthy and
honourable man in society, beyond the hope of redemption, and sink him
in infamy forever." After the jury deliberated for an hour, Carpenter was
found not guilty.[1]

In Tennessee, James Keyton, a white man, was indicted for the rape
of a slave girl.[2] Although Keyton was eventually acquitted, the records
reveal that in some states the law implied that, legally, a slave could be
raped. No records previous to the Civil War period show the conviction
of a white man for raping an enslaved woman.[3] If a white male assaulted
a slave woman, her owner might charge the assailant with assault and
battery, but the woman had no voice in the matter herself.

Also in Tennessee, Grandison, a slave, was convicted of an assault and
battery with the intent to ravish. But the initial court case failed to state
that the alleged victim, Mary Douglass, was a white woman, and the rape
of a white woman was considered to be punishable by hanging. Judge
Green delivered his opinion, "An assault on a black woman, with intent
to ravish, is not punished with death, as in the case of assault on the body
of a free white woman."[4] The ruling suggests that punishments other than
death could have been possible for the rape of a black woman, at least by
a slave.

A Missouri court reached a similar ruling when it could not decide
if Sophia Fulmar was a white woman. "Under *sec 1*... she would be a
mulatto, and the prisoner [a slave] could not be convicted capitally." The
same case also concluded, "Though the woman may be unchaste, '*or of
easy virtue*,' this is no justification of such assault upon her by a negro."[5]

Most states had laws stating that no crime of rape against slave women
existed. Slave women were regarded as chattel under the law. Some states,
like Louisiana, had laws that included free black women as well.[6] In 1859
Mississippi, a slave named George, was accused of raping a slave girl under the age of twelve. The counsel for the defendant made this statement:

> The crime of rape does not exist in this state between African
> slaves.... Their sexual intercourse is left to be regulated by
> their owners. The regulations of law, as to the white race, on
> the subject of sexual intercourse, do not and cannot, for obvi-
> ous reasons, apply to slaves; their intercourse is promiscuous,
> and the violation of a female slave by a male slave would be a
> mere assault and battery.

Judge Harris responded:

> With the exception of [four cases in Mississippi, Tennessee,

and North Carolina][7] founded mainly upon unmeaning twad-
dle, in which some humane judges and law writers have indulged, as to the influence of the "natural law," "civilization
and Christian enlightenment," in amending ... the rigor of the
common law, and on a supposed analogy between villanage
[feudalism] in England and slavery here, the cases and text-
writers are uniform in declaring that slavery, as it exists in this
country, was unknown to the common law of England, and
hence its provisions are inapplicable to the injuries inflicted
on the slaves here.

In other words, the law supported the position that slaves could not be
raped, and the defendant was released. A year later, the law was changed
to state that "the actual or attempted commission of a rape by a negro
or mulatto on a female negro or mulatto, under twelve years of age, is
punishable by death or whipping, as the jury may decide."[8]

Also in 1859, a Virginia slave was hanged for the rape of two young
girls, one white and the other black. The initial arrest warrant specifically stated "a negro female child."[9] Although the punishment would have
likely been less severe if a white child had not been involved, the warrant
demonstrates some states recognized that a black child could be raped.
In general, slaves were considered to be property and as such, white owners rarely sought compensation for the rape of a slave, especially when
most sexual assaults were carried out by the owners themselves or by
family members. Unlike that of a slave owner's wife or daughter, a slave's
reputation was not a factor. In fact, if a slave became pregnant from a
sexual assault, an owner could profit from the child.

Few records exist of black women, free or slave, in getting rape cases to
court before the Civil War. Rape accusations made by white women were
rarely taken seriously. Black women's voices generally went unheard. On
the other hand, the situation for black men was different. Whether they
were free or slaves, when accused of raping a white woman or girl, they
were often punished more severely than white men. As in other rape
cases, wealthy women were more likely to be taken seriously than poor
women.

One Virginia newspaper reported, "Hiram, a negro, belonging to Mrs.
Stephens of Green County, was tried ... for committing a rape on a respectable old lady of this county, and convicted. He was sentenced to be
hung." A subsequent article informed the public that the sentence had
indeed been carried out.[10]

In an instance from Kentucky, "a young lady, some fourteen or fifteen

years of age, was going home alone, when a negro man... stopped her
horse, dragged her from his back and ravished her—then taking a club
beat her over the head until he supposed her to be dead, and leaving her
in the road, fled." Another man discovered her and "called out a posse....
The negro was caught, and his captors had a fire built, intending to burn
him alive, when they changed their purpose and hung him on the spot. A
righteous punishment, say we," opined the *Richmond Daily Dispatch*.[11]

In most court cases, as in the trials of white men, proof of force was required. In 1832, a free black man by the name of Fields climbed into bed
with a white woman and raised her night garment. The action awakened
the woman, listed only as S.L. The jury found that Fields

> did not intend to have carnal knowledge... by force, but in-
> tended to have such carnal knowledge of her when she was
> asleep; that he made the attempt... when she was asleep, but
> used no force, except... getting to bed with her, and stripping
> up her night garment... which caused her to awake.

The Supreme Court of Virginia determined this action was not "an attempt to ravish" and acquitted Fields.[12]

The laws regarding the rape of girls were clearly different for black
and white men. In Arkansas, Mississippi, Tennessee, Texas, and Virginia,
slaves who were found guilty of raping a white child were sentenced to
death. White men in the same states received prison sentences of five to
twenty-one years.[13] Judge Manly urged lawmakers to consider lowering
the age for "races" originally from Africa:

> It is unquestionable that climate, food, clothing and the like,
> have a great influence on hastening physical development.
> Whether it may not be advisable to move down to an earlier
> age than 14, the period of puberty, for a portion, if not for all
> the elements in our population, may be a proper inquiry for
> the Statesman.[14]

Even though black men accused of rape or intent to commit rape
tended to receive harsher sentences if convicted, this was true of any
crime, not just rape. Some states allowed slaves to appeal, and many
questioned whether masters had the right to testify as a character witness
because of their monetary interest. An 1856 North Carolina case ruled
that a master could serve as a witness in capital cases. Judge Pearson

stated, "The testimony of the master cannot be excluded without man-
ifest inconsistency. The slave is put on trial as a *human being* entitled
to have his guilt or innocence passed on by a jury."[15] Despite the inconsistent treatment of blacks in general, a Louisiana court agreed: "Slaves
are prosecuted as persons, and they ought not to be deprived of the testimony of their owners, because a verdict may injure them in a pecuniary
way. The point at issue is not their value, but their guilt or innocence."[16]

Trials where the defendant's guilt was upheld still often cast doubt on a
woman's credibility. In North Carolina, Narcissa Craig delayed reporting
that she had been raped by a slave named Peter. Her father had been
away, and she claimed the defendant had raped her in her night clothes.
She cried out, but her cousin lived two hundred yards away. She failed
to report the incident until two weeks later because she was "afraid and
ashamed." Her aunt testified that Narcissa had indeed told her about
the rape and showed her the bloody garments. The defense attempted
to challenge Narcissa's testimony because she had failed to report the
incident promptly. Because of the delay, the attorney felt the act should
have been treated as consensual. Judge Pearson held the opinion that
silence on the victim's part after a rape did not always equate to consent:

> It is not *a rule of law* that silence . . . raises a presumption that
> the witness has sworn falsely. The passage in the books . . . use
> the word "presumption," not as a rule of law, but an inference
> of fact, and treat of *silence*, as a circumstance tending strongly
> to impeach the credibility of the witness; on the ground that a
> forcible violation of her person so outrages the female instinct,
> that a woman, not only will make an outcry for aid at the time,
> but will instantly, and involuntarily, after its perpetration, seek
> some one to whom she can make known the injury and give
> vent to her feelings . . . but it is no where held that this female
> instinct is so strong and unerring as to have been made the
> foundation of a rule of law.[17]

The judgment held, undoubtedly because the defendant was a slave.

As in rape trials where the alleged rapist was white, women who were
considered to be unchaste were believed less often. A Florida court gave a
stay of execution to a slave named Cato. Susan Leonard stated that Cato
entered her bedroom under darkness. "He bore down on my shoulder
and reached with his hand and got his knife and put his hand on my
forehead and bore my head back against my pillow, and drew the knife

across my throat." Fearful for her life, Susan was "afraid if I spoke or made any noise he would kill me; he then . . . had a connexion with me." A witness in the other room overheard Susan say, "Lord-a-mercy is that you Cato?"

The defense produced twelve witnesses stating that both women were "common prostitutes." Judge DuPont offered his opinion that

> *persuasion* not *force* was being used by the person to over-come her will and to accomplish his purpose. And if we con-nect this evidence with the testimony of the prosecutrix, it will be seen the effort at *persuasion* occurred subsequent to the *threat* testified to by her, for the purport of her evidence is that he made the threats to kill her *immediately* on her being aroused from sleep. Taking into consideration the degraded character of the witness, and she was *contradicted* in several important particulars of the other witness on the part of the State, we think that this case which eminently demanded that the question of *force* and *violence* should have been kept di-rectly before the minds of the jury.[18]

Sir Matthew Hale's aforementioned words of warning that rape was "an accusation easily to be made and hard to be proved, and harder to be defended by the party accused, though never so innocent," were repeated and Cato was awarded a new trial.

Other judges seemed to sympathize with black men being accused of rape. In 1852, Judge Lumpkin said:

> The crime from the very nature of it, is calculated to excite indignation in every heart; and when perpetrated by a slave on a free white female of immature mind and body, that indigna-tion becomes greater, and is more difficult to repress. The very helplessness of the accused, however, like infancy and woman-hood, appeals to our sympathy.[19]

Lumpkin's supposed sympathy was not enough to overrule the previous court's finding of guilt. The defendant was executed.

In the early part of the nineteenth century, slaves convicted of rape or attempted rape were generally executed in Virginia. By the 1840s, a higher percentage were transported out of state instead. By the time of the Civil War, the percentage had increased yet again.[20] One slave, John, was initially convicted to hang for attempting to commit rape, "but the sentence was commuted to transportation."[21]

As has already been pointed out, black men convicted of rape generally faced capital punishment. White men usually served prison sentences. However, the trials themselves functioned in much the same way, centering around the man's use of force and the woman's resistance and consent.

Rape during War

Until recent years, documentation of rape during war was rare. Not until World War I did any serious record keeping begin.[22] During modern warfare, raped women generally have refused to discuss the assault due to shame and humiliation. In the Bosnian conflict, Muslim women felt that to be raped was a "fate worse than death" due to the patriarchal culture that expected women to maintain their purity.[23] These present-day attitudes demonstrate a haunting similarity to those of the Civil War era.

Historically, rape during war has been a way to humiliate the enemy and despoil his property. A raped woman was often regarded as unmarriageable. As her father's property, she became worthless. Her "protector" had failed in his role. Women were also easy targets for racial or ethnic hatred. Rapes by encroaching armies caused collective fear within communities. Once women's areas came under the invader's control, women could be used at the attacker's whim. Rape in war was made easier by the rarity of punishment.

During the American Revolution, the Connecticut towns of Fairfield and New Haven were raided by English and Hessian troops. A couple of women fought off sexual assaults; another was gang-raped. In 1776, New Jersey and Staten Island fared worse. Rape was a symbol of power for the victorious side. British troops gang-raped numerous women. Some were held hostage for days. Officers went "about the town by night, entering into houses and openly inquiring for women."[24] While stationed at Staten Island, Lord Francis Rawdon joked in a letter to the Earl of Huntingdon that because the soldiers were as "riotous as satyrs" a girl could not "step into the bushes ... without running the risk of being ravished ... and of consequence we have most entertaining courts martial every day." He went on to comment that a woman to the "southward" behaved much better after "having been forced by seven of our men" because she didn't complain about "their usage," even though she had "despised" it.[25]

British historian Arnold Toynbee documented incidents of rape by German soldiers in Belgium and France during World War I. In Belgium, "a girl of sixteen was violated by six soldiers and bayonetted in five places for offering resistance. Her parents were kept off with rifles." In France, a woman was raped "in the presence of her four-year-old child." In another instance, after a group of soldiers broke into a house, they tied the owner. His wife escaped through a window, but "four soldiers followed her and violated her in turn. Two other soldiers violated this lady's niece, aged thirteen." Another woman was "eighty-nine years old and died of the effects," and a girl went "out of her mind—she had been violated by a number of Germans in succession." These examples are only a sampling of the assaults Toynbee recorded.[26]

Another author wrote about the rapes in Bailleul, France:

> There were at least thirty cases of outrages on girls and young unmarried women, authenticated by sworn statements of witnesses and generally by medical certificates of injury. It is extremely probable that, owing to the natural reluctance of women to give evidence... the actual number... largely exceeds this. At least five officers were guilty of such offences... daughters were outraged in the presence of their mothers, and mothers in the presence of their little children.... A young girl of nineteen was violated by one officer while the other held her throat and pointed a revolver, after which the two officers exchanged their respective roles. The officers and soldiers usually hunted in couples, either entering the houses under the pretence of seeking billets [lodging] or forcing the doors by open violence.[27]

Following the war, several notable authors dismissed such accounts as mere propaganda.

During World War II, rape involving German and Japanese soldiers tended to be mentioned the most often. However, before a campaign, U.S. Army General George Patton Jr. stated, "I then told him that, in spite of my most diligent efforts, there would unquestionably be some raping, and that I should like to have the details as early as possible so that the offenders could be properly hanged."[28] Only with the publication of criminology professor J. Robert Lilly's *Taken by Force* in 2007 has anyone studied the rapes committed by American GIs in serious detail. As in the Civil War records, a higher percentage of black men than white men were prosecuted and hanged. Lilly separated the statistics by country—England, France, and Germany—to evaluate the different types of rape as well as the numbers involved.

In England, Lilly categorized rapes as acquaintance, partial stranger, and stranger rape. Acquaintance rape pertained to people who had met and had some knowledge of each other, but whose contact had been limited. These cases were the least prosecuted. Partial stranger rapes referred to when the victim had seen the attacker in the past, but did not know him. This type of case was prosecuted slightly more often than acquaintance rapes. The most commonly prosecuted type was stranger rape where neither the victim nor her attacker had met before. In more than half of the rapes, alcohol was involved, and weapons were used around 40 percent of the time. Weapons included fists, knives, guns, sticks, and bottles.[29]

In France, during active combat conditions, Lilly recorded that the number of rapes that included brutality increased. More than half were stranger rape. Surprisingly, most of the soldiers tried for rape were *not* men involved in active combat.[30] Weapons were used in all but a small fraction of the French cases. Women often fought their attackers, which supported their innocence and virtue in American eyes.[31] In Germany, Lilly's statistics showed that 70 percent of the cases were stranger rape. The brutality of the attacks increased as well as the number of groups of raiding soldiers, who wandered the countryside alerting other soldiers where to find women.[32] The use of alcohol in rape cases declined from cases in other countries.

This study of other wars relates to the Civil War by demonstrating that rapes are rarely reported during wartime. To ignore this fact contributes to a lack of understanding about the crime and war itself. Rape often reaches epidemic proportions during wartime. The war atmosphere creates conditions that makes rape easy with little likelihood of punishment. Rape is common when men view their victims as vulnerable, such as when either party is intoxicated or when women lack male protectors.

In 1863, Union Major-General William S. Rosecrans wrote about wartime conditions in his report from Tennessee to Secretary of War E. M. Stanton:

> The crimes of spying, murder, arson, rape, and others ... are increasing, and the power to check them by inflicting the penalty of death is a nullity, for the delays necessary to get them a regular trial by general court-martial, and holding them

General William S. Rosecrans

until the matter is reviewed and approved by the President, such a time elapses that the troops are relieved and the culprit escapes. This ought to be remedied.[33]

Most convictions for rape during the Civil War took place during times of occupation, not under actual battle conditions. Courts-martial were generally held near the location of the crime. Soldiers had more time on their hands during occupation, as did the military authorities, who would have been responsible for gathering the necessary five to thirteen officers to convene a court. At times of heavy fighting, circumstances would have challenged authorities in locating the required number of officers for judges. Also, a woman who had been raped would have had difficulty finding the appropriate official in order to report the crime.

During wartime, the plight of women is often overlooked, discounted as exaggeration, or dismissed as propaganda. As the next chapter will show, the same can be said for the Civil War.

Chapter Three

"So Much For a Dreadful Outrage"

An Overview of Rape in the Civil War

S IR LEON RADZINOWICZ, A PROMINENT University of Cambridge criminol-
ogist, stated in the twentieth century that the number of all crimes
recorded were a mere fraction of those that had actually taken place; sexual assaults during wartime even more so. Using Radzinowicz's premise,
J. Robert Lilly determined by mathematical formula the approximate
number of American rapists and their victims during WWII. The basis
of the formula claims that 5 percent of rapes committed get reported.[1]

Approximately 450 cases of rape or attempted rape have been uncovered from Union military courts during the Civil War period. Applying
Lilly's formula, the number of soldiers accused of rape translates to approximately nine thousand. However, it should be noted most of the Confederate records have been lost. No one will ever know for certain how
many records have been lost on both sides. If the figure of nine thousand
is a close approximation to the actual numbers, the Civil War might be
regarded as a "low-rape" war, but the definition by historians of what con-
stitutes low rape has never been determined. Whether the figure is even
close to the actual number of rapes that took place is anyone's guess.
With rape rarely reported during the era, *any* figure is meaningless.

The war atmosphere created a fear of rape, and throughout the South,
women wrote about it. Catherine Devereux, the wife of a prominent
planter from North Carolina, wrote in her diary, "Butler sent out a foraging party into the Northern Neck, Negroes under a white officer. Details of the outrage of *twenty five* ladies by that band alone have been

Rose Greenhow and daughter at Old Capitol Prison

filed in Richmond!"[2] A daughter of a wealthy planter in South Carolina, Emma Holmes, wrote, "Fire, desolation, destruction of all property unremovable—all provisions, cattle & negroes carried—the rape and
consequent death or insanity of many ladies of the best families."[3]

Another plantation woman from Georgia, Mary Ann Jones, wrote,
"Squads of Yankees came all day. . . . The women finding it entirely unsafe
for them to be out of the house at all, would run in & conceal themselves
in our dwelling."[4] From Mississippi, Roxanna Cole wrote a letter to another family member: "Poor sister Martha. She, too, like me, had feared
the worst. I should have not suffered so that night had I known that mere

robbery was all I had to fear, but I had seen and heard so much of their lawless deed and worse threats that we knew not what to fear."[5]

Rose Greenhow, held as a Confederate spy, reported from Old Capitol Prison that

> for a period of seven days I, with my little child, was placed absolutely at the mercy of men without character or responsibility; that during the first evening a portion of these men became brutally drunk, and boasted in my hearing of the "nice times" they were expected to have with the female prisoners; and that rude violence was used towards a colored servant girl during that evening.[6]

Women's fears have been claimed to be unsubstantiated hearsay, but men made similar observations. Journalist George Augustus Sala wrote in his memoir of "the cattle and horses that have been carried off; the whole cities and villages that have been destroyed; of women ravished."[7] In August of 1863, Green Berry Samuels wrote in a letter to his wife, "We daily hear of deeds that would make a devil blush to commit; a few days since four young ladies of Loudoun Co. [Virginia] were violated in their beds at home."[8] The *Richmond Daily Dispatch* also reported the incident: "Three sisters... have been made the victims of their [Union soldiers'] lust, because a brother of theirs was a Captain in the Confederate service. A short time since they attempted to outrage the person of a wife of a clergyman, who is also in our service."[9]

John Beauchamp Jones, a Confederate war clerk, received a dispatch from Union General Benjamin Butler:

> An attempt was made this morning by private Roucher... to commit a rape upon the persons of Mrs. Minzer and Mrs. Anderson...
>
> On the outrage being discovered, he broke through the picket line, and fled for your lines. Our soldiers chased him, but were unable to overtake him.
>
> I have therefore the honor to request that you will return him, that I may inflict the punishment which his dastardly offense merits. I cannot be responsible for the good conduct of my soldiers, *if they are to find protection from punishment by entering your lines.*[10]

Apparently on the same evening, Private Peter Rausher of the 5th Pennsylvania Cavalry had allegedly entered the home of Rebecca Good, where her sister Sarah answered the door. Rausher asked her, "Where is that man who just came in?" Sarah wondered what man, and he explained that the guards had said a man had come into her house. She assured him there was no man, only her sister and little children. They then sat across from each other inside the house and talked. When Rausher put his arms around her neck and kissed her, she pushed him away and he threatened her with his rifle. Sarah hid under the bed. When she came out, Rausher grabbed her dress. She screamed and he ran off. Two other witnesses from the 5th Pennsylvania Cavalry heard the scream.

Rausher was acquitted on both charges of assault with intent to commit rape and desertion, due to a lack of evidence.[11] The records remain silent as to whether General Butler incorrectly named the women in the dispatch, or if more women were involved than the two in the court-martial transcript. It also remains puzzling as to why, if numerous soldiers gave chase to Rausher, they were not called for the hearing.

General Butler had his own history regarding the topic of rape. During the occupation of New Orleans, the local women repeatedly insulted Union soldiers. Butler responded by issuing General Order No. 28: "When any female shall by word, gesture, or movement insult or show contempt for any officer or soldier of the United States, she shall be regarded and held liable to be treated as a woman of the town plying her avocation."[12]

Although the order is phrased in euphemisms, it meant that women who insulted Union soldiers were to be considered whores and allowed to be raped. No known rape cases have surfaced as a result of the order, but women would have been reluctant to report any assaults when the men had been given permission to do as they pleased. Even if no rapes occurred, the fact remains that the threat of rape was used as a war tactic against Southern women.

The *Official Records* are riddled with numerous reports of plundering, arson, rape, ravishing, and great outrages against women. Yet only the crimes against women have been dismissed as being rare. If rape was unlikely to have been reported and prosecuted during peacetime, it remains inconceivable the crime would have been prosecuted more harshly during wartime.

During a murder investigation in Virginia, William D. Wallach claimed that "a small party of deserters from the Union forces . . . were roaming that region with arms in their hands, entering the houses, marauding and ravishing in the neighborhood. They had ravished two respectable females."[13] Major General Darius N. Couch reported from North Carolina,

"Women are ravished and robbed by stragglers all over the country."[14] Some historians consider Couch to be a cautious general, others believe he was calculating. More importantly, he would have unlikely sensationalized the incidence of rape in an official report.

Lieutenant Daniel D. Lynn, 6th U.S. Infantry wrote from California that "white men at the South Fork had whipped and raped Indian women."[15] From Summersville in western Virginia (present-day West Virginia), Brigadier General John B. Floyd said that "thefts, plunder, arson, and rape are occuring every day."[16] Colonel H. Haupt filed a report from Virginia: "Guerrillas are forming in various parts of the country, provoked by rapes and other crimes committed by Union men."[17] From Missouri, Major Austin A. King sent a report to General Rosecrans: "An inquiry by an honest military court into these things will develop the enormity of crimes of the most startling character. Robbery, murder, arson, and rapes will figure largely in the catalogue."[18]

In Alabama, several charges were brought against Russian immigrant, Colonel J.B. Turchin, of the 19th Illinois Regiment for neglect of duty in "the sack of Athens." Among the incidents, a group of his command went into the house of Milly Ann Clayton. They destroyed clothing and bed clothes. After threatening to shoot Milly Ann, they proceeded to the kitchen and attempted to rape a black servant.

Another squad of Turchin's soldiers plundered John F. Malone's house and law office. A part of this brigade went to Malone's plantation, where they "quartered in the negro huts for weeks, debauching the females." To pretend all of the women went willingly would be turning a blind eye to reality. And at the house of widow Charlotte Hine "a colored girl" was raped.[19] Private Ayer Bowers was identified as the rapist. Because the victim had been raped in front of her mistress, she had a white witness.[20]

Major General O. M. Mitchel, in charge of the brigade, filed a report with Secretary of War E. M. Stanton. He complained that his line extended more than 400 miles. "The most terrible outrages—robberies, rapes, arson, and plundering—are being committed by lawless brigands and vagabonds connected with the army." He went on to state that "wherever I am present in person all is quiet and orderly. . . . I beg authority to control these plunderers by visiting upon their crimes the punishment of death."[21] Apparently, Stanton granted Mitchel's request, but nothing changed.

Colonel J. S. Norton of the 21st Ohio Regiment submitted a deposition to the Committee on the Conduct of the War: "I charge Colonel Turchin, and the officers and soldiers of his command, with having committed outrages and depredations upon the people of Limestone county... with committing rapes upon servant girls in the presence of their mistresses."[22] The committee took no action. Because Norton had violated normal military protocol, he was relieved of command. Formal charges were filed against Turchin.

Charlotte Hine testified on behalf of her unnamed servant. Normally Charlotte had been unafraid of soldiers coming to her house. She often gave them milk for which they offered to pay. On May 3, 1862, a few soldiers came to her house and stole some meat from her smokehouse. The following day, three men returned and "at once commenced indecent familiarities with them [the slaves], calling the women, 'Sissy,' and throwing their arms around them, running their hands into their bosoms."[23] The soldiers rummaged through some drawers and searched the house before going outside, where they went after the women again. According to Charlotte, "all had left the place, except for one woman and her daughter, the latter about 14 years of age." The girl held a baby, and one of the soldiers told her to put the child down. He said, "I want to use you." When the girl's mother screamed for help from Charlotte, the girl cried for her mother. The soldier threatened, "God damn your mammy, we will have her next."

Charlotte ran into the yard and "there before me a horrid outrage was committed on her person by the man, and afterward the outrage was repeated by one of the others, but not by the third man." As for the girl's mother, "I locked [her] up in a closet, but let her out to escape them, and she ran away into the thicket. They tried to hunt her up."

Another officer stated, "Col. Turchin asked me if I had the man under arrest. I replied... I would not arrest one of my men on negro testimony."[24] Private Bowers, the soldier accused of raping the girl, was sent to the guardhouse for two weeks before returning to duty.[25] The second man seems to have escaped charges completely.

A *New York Times* article denied any wrongdoing: "In General Mitchel's invasion of Alabama and Georgia, one of his officers, Turchin, allowed his men to sack a village... and to ravish a whole seminary of young ladies! The whole foundation of this story is this: Our men captured the village." After a battle, the soldiers began to burn houses. "On the investigation before the Court-martial, the only woman injured was a negro prostitute, who was thought not to have been especially unwilling. So much for dreadful outrage."[26]

The reporter first resorted to propaganda, then turned around and pretended that no women had been raped. The single case that made it to the court-martial records was dismissed entirely as being brought by a prostitute. Had the reporter read the real record he might have thought differently, but the truth of the matter is that few during the era treated the rape of black or poor women as a matter of any importance.

Not only did some officers ignore the rapes their men committed, some allegedly perpetrated the act themselves. A Maine volunteer wrote in his diary from Virginia:

> At this place occurred a dastardly outrage, if [the] report be true. Colonel Byles, of the 99th Penn. and his ADJT [adjutant] made their headquarters at a farm house near by occupied by two women alone. They made infamous proposals to them, which being refused, these miserable, cowardly skulks threatened to burn the house unless their demands were complied with. So to save their home, and themselves from being turned out into the "bleak December," they submitted.
>
> Had this outrage been the work of privates, they would probably have dangled from the nearest tree in very short order, Col Byles consenting thereto. But there may be another side to the story, women are not *all* of them *always* paragons of virtue and these innocent creatures may have been "as deep in the mud as Col Byles was in the mire." As who shall say?
>
> One thing we did know, Old Byles, was a drunken old fool and one never knows when an officer keeps in this condition, what crazy and dirty ideas may creep into his brain.[27]

The private responded in a typical period style by questioning the women's reputations, but not only was Colonel Edwin Ruthin Biles never investigated for improper conduct or possible rape, he mustered out on July 1, 1865, as a brigadier general.

In a letter to his wife, Confederate soldier Sergeant Edwin Fay wrote that "there were two beautiful young ladies near Vicksburg, they [Union soldiers] took two negro women in the parlor before their mistresses and sent in soldier after soldier till they had actually killed the negro women by *violation*."[28] While Fay seemed more sympathetic to the women who had to watch the assaults, two women were raped to death. The symbolism is all too obvious. In the first instance, white women were forced to watch the rapes of their slaves. The soldiers conveniently chose black women where they were far less likely to be prosecuted for the crime. In doing so, they maintained white female purity, all the while proving that the white women could have been the victims if the soldiers had chosen to do so.

Besides letters, diaries, and the *Official Records*, newspapers reported rapes that have been referred to as unsubstantiated accounts or propaganda. While newspaper pieces about rape have certainly been used as propaganda to motivate soldiers to fight for both sides during the war, most articles were about specific incidents.

According to the *Arkansas True Democrat*, two Union soldiers "seized two young girls and outraged them. Afterwards, two negroes, after severe struggling committed rapes on two respectable ladies, while their white comrades in arms stood by laughing at the shrieks and prayers of the poor women." Less than a month before, the same paper had reported that several officers entered the house of Mr. Anthony:

> [They] permitted a number of negro teamsters to seize the daughters... and ravish these unprotected females.[29] Their mother besought the protection of the officers, but these brutal men cursed her as a d___d rebel, saying that they understood that the husbands of her daughters were in the Confederate service, and they were being served properly thus to be outraged by a race they had enslaved.[30]

Again the symbolism is unmistakable. In these cases, the white soldiers took no risk by letting the black men do the raping. Yet they were equally guilty by allowing the rapes to happen. In fact, the brutality of war is particularly apparent where the white soldiers stood by and laughed or essentially told the women they deserved rape by association with their husbands in the Confederate military.

In West Virginia, in another rape by association, Northern soldiers raped the wife of a state legislature representative, who had voted for secession. "Mrs. Hall had her clothing tied over her head ... and was thrust into the street.... Report says an outrage, to which death is preferable, was perpetrated upon her person."[31]

From Virginia:

> Two young ladies... were seized by a squad of the enemy who invaded the residence, forced into a chamber and their maiden persons violated by the fiends incarnate in the presence of

their parents, who could do nothing but implore the wretches to kill them and commute a fate worse than death.[32]

In other words, raped women became unmarriageable damaged goods, property that was no longer useful to the men in their families.

In Palmyra, Missouri, after the disappearance of a Union sympathizer, Colonel John McNeil decided to shoot ten prisoners in ten days if the man was not returned. U.S. Provost Marshal W.R. Strachan, acting for McNeil, published the notice in the *Missouri Courier*. Mary Humphrey, the wife of one of the condemned men, went to Strachan on the morning her husband was to be shot. She told him that "if her husband should be murdered she would be unable to support her children, and begged... to release him from the sentence. Strachan at first refused, but the poor woman's importunities were so persistent that he finally told her if she would raise him $500 and permit him to use her, he would release her husband." Mary raised the money by canvassing the town. "Strachan pocketed it, compelled the poor woman to submit to his hellish lust, and released her husband."[33] Strachan was found guilty of using his office for an immoral purpose—not rape, which would have been a characteristic finding for the era.[34] Even though Mary had been coerced, she had given her consent.

Ironically, the *New York Times* claimed that the Palmyra Massacre was justified, as the men involved "*were guerrillas*... murdering helpless, unarmed men, ravishing women, burning houses."[35] Apparently the correspondent was of the opinion that rape was all right if the women were Confederate women. Strachan was fined $680 for embezzlement and extortion and sentenced to a year in prison. Major General Rosecrans disapproved the sentence and pardoned Strachan with an honorable release.[36]

Also in Missouri, when a female soldier's gender was discovered, a comrade attempted to rape her. She responded by shooting him. "I meant to disable his arm, but he stooped so quick that the ball entered his face and found its way under his skull-cap." Instead of being angry with him, she tended him until he was out of danger. As a result, he sent her a written apology, "very humble, and begging forgiveness in such a manner that I forgave him."[37]

In Maryland, two reports varied on an incident involving General Daniel Sickles. "Sickles's soldiers have already violated three of the most respectable ladies in the lower counties. He [the correspondent] told me their names. One of them I knew. She is about 16."[38] In addition, "a party of Sickles's 'dead rabbits,' who had been turned loose upon the unfortunate populace in lower Maryland, burned the homestead of a wealthy citizen, turned his family out into the fields, and worse than all, carried off one of the young ladies to their den, where she was outraged by nine of the devils."[39]

Dead Rabbits were New York City gang members from the time period, and General Daniel Sickles had a history of public scandals, both before and during the war. One scandal included shooting and killing his wife's lover, Philip Barton Key II, son of Francis Scott Key. During the ensuing trial, Sickles was the first person in U.S. history to plead innocent due to temporary insanity. In another scandal, he escorted a prostitute by the name of Fanny White into the chambers of the New York State Assembly. He was reprimanded for the act. Later, Fanny White accompanied Sickles to England. He left his pregnant wife at home and presented White to Queen Victoria, using as an alias the surname of a New York political opponent.[40] In the reported wartime attacks, a commander with such little respect for women was unlikely to have treated rape harshly. More importantly, the conflicting reports tell us very little about how many women were actually raped.

Several fathers were killed while trying to protect their daughters from rape. Captain Samuel Holley's house "was invaded by a lot of Yankee officers and men, who introduced themselves by a brutal proposition to Capt. H's two daughters.... While endeavoring to accomplish their designs by force, the indignant father shot one of the demons dead, and had taken aim at another, when he was instantly killed."[41]

Likewise, John Patrick had been killed the week before in an attempt "to save an only and beloved daughter from a fate worse than death." Dr. Thomas R. Dunn "died in defence of his much beloved daughter, who was being outraged by a Yankee officer. He killed the monster, but was in turn killed himself."[42]

In Fauquier County, Virginia, Union officers occupied the house of Dr. Shumate. A major decided to make the doctor's daughter the object of his attraction.

> [He] made several vain attempts to enter the sleeping apartment of the young lady, when the outrage reaching the ears of the father, he told the scoundrel that another such attempt would cost him his life.... In spite of this fair caution, the God forsaken wretch again attempted to accomplish his diabolical design, when, true to his word, Dr. Shumate sped a

ball through his craven heart... the Major's companions—all officers—fell upon the Doctor... riddling his body with bullets.[43]

All of the reports mention beautiful or much beloved daughters; the men were respectable citizens. In fact, most newspapers reported wealthy women and/or respectable women. Poor and black women were less likely to be considered newsworthy.

During General William T. Sherman's occupation of Georgia and the Carolinas, a private complained that women had emptied chamber pots on the passing soldiers and the men "did not respect girls who emptied chamber pots." He then stated the women were "spanked" on "bare flesh," but he "never saw or personally knew of a woman being insulted or abused by a Yankee." Some soldiers claimed that women were treated with kindness. An officer reported, "The war is with men and their property, but women are always treated with respect." He continued that crimes were "falsely charged to the Union foragers." Another colonel said, "The persons of women, it is my belief, have very seldom been molested, and I have been in a position to know about this."[44]

Newspaper reports suggest such idyllic treatment may have not been the case. In Holly Springs before the taking of Atlanta, Sherman's men went to the home of "a highly respectable and intelligent lady.... A squad of some dozen or more of the hellish fiends forcibly entered her house, and in the presence of her screaming little children, outraged her person."[45] The number of soldiers involved may have been exaggerated in the report, but it clearly states that a woman was gang-raped in front of her children.

At least two rape/murders seem to have taken place in Georgia. Sherman's soldiers, "after expelling the father and mother from their home, violated the person of the daughter... seventeen years of age. The dead body of the girl was found in the house by some of our scouts."[46]

And in another case, "a body of Yankees went to the residence of Mr. Wm. Iverson." After plundering the household, the soldiers "laid hands on his daughter (about 16 years of age) and by force, one after another, satisfy[ed] their hellish lust." The girl's father attempted to get his daughter away from the soldiers, but they beat him with clubs. She died before the soldiers left. "The Yankees came back next morning and dug a hole near the well, in the yard, and put the corpse in and covered it."[47]

Near Atlanta before the infamous March to the Sea, the *Charleston Mercury* reported that Union soldiers "seized five negro women, and in the yard, in the presence of the white family... they violated their persons. In one neighborhood... they violated the persons of six respectable ladies."[48] While the numbers may or may not be exaggerated, rapes appear to have taken place.

During the March to the Sea from Clinton, Georgia, "clothes [were] taken off the backs of some contrabands [escaped slaves], and female servants taken and violated without mercy, by their officers." From Milledgeville, Georgia: "The most dreadful thing was their violence to the ladies. At least six or seven suffered the last extremity. One young girl became crazed in consequence, and has been sent to the Asylum." Another newspaper reported the same attack: "We are informed that the incarnate devils ravished some of the nicest ladies in town. We pen the paragraph with horror. Our blood runs cold as we write." The correspondent also stated about the woman committed to the asylum that "her reason tottered beneath the load of wounded honor, and the poor victim is ruined forever."[49] At least one Union soldier claimed the articles were propaganda. "These miserable and deluded people read and believe all these stories and the poor women are frightened nearly to death."[50]

The *New York Times* also denied that any such conduct took place. "There is little truth in any such statements, and that little may be aptly illustrated from *Don Juan*."[51] The reports from Southern newspapers were written in typical period style. The articles were certainly meant to anger Confederate soldiers over the idea that women had been raped. However, the dismissal in Northern newspapers is the same denial put forth by some modern historians. Women were raped, and it was common for white victims to be ostracized. If such a victim was suddenly considered valueless to society, it is hardly surprising that she would have been sent to an asylum. And most rapes of the poor white and black women would have gone unreported completely.

When Sherman turned his army toward the Carolinas, Sergeant Arthur McCarty of the 78th Ohio was court-martialed for the rape of a teenage girl. Three Illinois men discovered McCarty on top of Martha Clowell, who was crying for her mother. Upon being seen, McCarty quickly stood and buttoned his pants.

The men failed to arrest him because McCarty claimed to have paid her "a quarter of a dollar in Silver" for sexual favors. In his defense, McCarty said the house had come recommended to him "as one occupied by women of bad repute" and that the girl had screamed when the other men arrived unannounced. As was fairly common when rapes occured during troop movements, the regiment was 100 miles away from where the allegation had taken place, and the victim never testified.

McCarty was found guilty and sentenced to two years, hard labor. A petition from the regiment with more than fifty names attesting to McCarty's good character were sent to the president. Another letter, signed by Captain William McCarty (a relative, perhaps?), stated that McCarty had always been an excellent soldier. In addition, McCarty himself sent the president a letter in which his story from the court-martial shifted dramatically. He said the men who had given testimony against him at the court-martial had conspired against him. He and another corporal had originally approached the Clowell house when three men were already there. He named the men who had testified against him. No sexual connection, consensual or otherwise, was mentioned. President Johnson pardoned McCarty, and he returned to the regiment.[52]

In Columbia, South Carolina, Mrs. T.B.C. was seized by an officer, dragged by her hair, and thrown to the floor. She pleaded with him by holding up her infant child and begging him to spare her. In her place, the officer raped her maid.[53]

Though the reports are "sketchy," real rape did occur. In a time when such a crime was rarely reported, newspaper accounts and official records were likely to have only skimmed the surface. For the most part, only well-off white women were taken seriously, and black women generally required a white witness to be believed.

Chapter Four

"She Made All the Resistance in Her Power"

Black Soldiers Who Received the Death Penalty

RAPE WAS A CAPITAL CRIME during the Civil War era, and nearly thirty U.S. soldiers were executed for rape or attempted rape. More than half of those who received the death sentence were black. Black soldiers constituted 10 percent of the approximate 2.1 million Union soldiers. Even though black men were prosecuted more harshly for rape than white men, few were actually executed for the crime. This chapter focuses on the black soldiers who received the death penalty.

In Dixon County, Tennessee, on November 13, 1863, Indiana Rose rode her mare along the "pike." When she was about a mile from home, Private George Nelson of the 13th United States Colored Troops (USCT) halted her and questioned her about where she had been and what business she had there. He proceeded to ask where she lived. After Indiana's response, Nelson informed her that she would need to accompany him as he "had a fight with some rebels" near her home. Indiana refused to go with him. Nelson drew his gun with the threat that he would shoot her. Two other men joined Nelson, and Indiana went with Nelson, begging for him to let her go.

Nelson drew a bayonet and warned her that if she resisted accompanying him into the woods, he would run her through. She started crying and they threatened to hang her. Nelson cocked his gun and forced her into the woods. Once there, he threw her to the ground and raped her. Afterward, he stole her money, a dollar and a half, but the other men ordered him to return it. Daniel Tierce was the second man to rape her, and Lewis Hardin the third. Hardin asked Indiana if she was hurt after the attack.

"I was near killed," she replied. She also believed that Hardin would have let her go if the other men had not threatened to shoot him. Hardin's afterthought response was not atypical for a man involved in gang rape during wartime. He may have been representative of a man who would not ordinarily rape during peacetime but went along with the group out of fear.

During Tierce's court-martial, Indiana was asked, "Did this man use force to throw you upon the ground and did you use your utmost endeavors to prevent him executing his desires, or did you simply cry out, thus yielding a tacit consent?" As in civilian cases, a woman had to fight with the utmost resistance or she was considered not to have been raped.

In this particular case, only the ringleader, Nelson, was sentenced to be executed. However, he managed to escape and was recaptured while waiting for sentencing. Lewis Hardin and Daniel Tierce were sentenced to dishonorable discharges and ten and twelve years, hard labor respectively. Hardin received an order for release from prison after serving two years. No further record on Tierce was found.[1]

In April 1865, after being informed that only women were present at the house of Fanny Crawford, several men went to her home near Richmond, Virginia. Sergeant Danbridge Brooks knocked on the door and demanded that Fanny open it. When she failed to let the men enter, he kicked the door, breaking the latch. Fanny ran upstairs and screamed from the window.

Brooks said, "Shoot her—shoot her." Corporal John Sheppard fired a pistol in her direction. Along with Brooks and Sheppard, Sergeant William Jackson and Private John Adams broke down the door and entered the Crawford residence. They looted a bureau and several storage trunks. Jackson carried Fanny into the hallway and raped her. From the bedroom, she heard the screams of her thirteen-year-old niece, Eliza Woodson. Brooks threatened Eliza with a gun, threw her on the bed, and raped her in front of her eight-year-old brother while Sheppard remained in the doorway and watched.

After the assault, Eliza scrambled to the floor, but one of the men returned her to the bed. "I tried to keep him from pulling my legs open," she stated.

Sheppard warned her that "if she didn't hush her noise, he would shoot her." He then raped her. As soon as he finished his attack on Eliza, he went into the hallway where Jackson held Fanny on the floor. Jackson left the passageway, and Sheppard proceeded to rape his second victim.

Afterward, the men made off with their booty of gloves, vests, a couple of small silver items, towels, an overcoat, and eight pounds of butter. Back at camp, the men bragged about their escapades to several comrades. Sheppard said that he "fucked the old woman, and the young one too." For their crimes, Sheppard, Brooks, and Jackson were hanged. The fourth man, Private John Adams, eluded capture.[2]

On June 8, 1864, teamster Robert Henry Hughes went to the home of Emily Batkins in Virginia and asked for something to eat. The cook, Eliza Jordan, baked and served some bread. A short time later, he helped himself to a plate of butter, a bowl of milk, and a knife. After eating, he searched the house. When he finished searching the main house, he continued on to the outhouses and Eliza's house.

Emily and Eliza joined Emily's daughter, Lucy, on the porch. Together, the frightened women kept tabs on Hughes's movements. Upon his return from Eliza's house, he grabbed the bottom of Lucy's dress and tried to raise it. She threatened to call a guard. Hughes pressed a bayonet against her side and stated that if she said another word, he would run her through. Before she could react, he caught her by the waist and threw her to the ground in the yard. Emily ran over to help her daughter and tried to pull him off Lucy. Eliza went for help, and two soldiers came to the women's aid. Hughes fled for cover in the woods, but the cavalrymen quickly caught up with him.

Hughes was tried for assault and battery with intent to commit rape and marauding to the prejudice of good order and military discipline. Found guilty on both charges, he was sentenced to hang. General George Meade stated, "The discipline of this army requires that an example be made of offenders of this class."[3]

After sentencing, Hughes admitted that his real name was William Johnson and that he had deserted from the 23rd USCT. On June 21, Johnson was escorted to the scaffold to the tune of the dead march. A white flag was displayed in full view of the enemy. Johnson admitted his guilt and was hung, "doubtless to prove the severity with which we treat offenders of this kind while in the enemy's country."[4] The historical record is unclear as to whether he was made an example because he was black, because he had attempted to rape a well-off white woman, because he had used an alias after desertion, or for all three reasons.

Florence Mew's father had taken the oath of allegiance to the Union and been promised protection from plundering soldiers. The promise was short-lived. On the night of August 20, 1865, in McPhersonville, South Carolina, a gang of six or seven soldiers from the 104th USCT ransacked his home. The group tied the two men present, then at gunpoint, with death threats, the women were escorted to a bedroom.

Florence and her mother jumped out an open window. Private James Grippen followed the women and chased Florence around the yard. He caught her dress and nearly tore it from her body. He then carried Florence into the house and raped her. According to Florence's testimony, two other men also raped her. One soldier offered his protection from further harm after doing so. Grippen later denied his presence and stated that he had been in another part of the house at the time of the rape.

On the same night, the gang burned Mary Heape's house, beat her son, and raped her daughter Euselia while Mary watched in horror. Private Benjamin Redding was accused of the assault. In addition to Euselia, he was charged with the rape of Florence and another woman by the name of Mary McTier, who never testified nor was her relationship given. Mary Heape testified that she believed Redding was innocent of raping her daughter, although he had stood by without offering assistance while two other men raped her. Even then, the court asked if her daughter had given resistance to the men's assaults.

"She made all the resistance in her power," Mary replied. She had begged the soldiers to stop their attacks, but they threatened to shoot her. Euselia Heape remained uncertain whether Redding was one of the men who had attacked her, and Florence Mew failed to recognize him as she had Grippen. Redding denied taking part in the rapes, though he admitted to being present. Grippen was found guilty of ransacking Mew's house and raping Florence Mew. Redding was found guilty of ransacking, but not guilty for any of the rapes. Instead, he was found guilty for aiding and abetting the rapes. Both were hanged for their crimes.[5] Two other privates, Gabriel Richardson and Isau Tobey, were found guilty for ransacking and put to hard labor for the rest of their enlistments. They were given dishonorable discharges. The remaining gang members, Howard Dixon and Henry Davis, were released from confinement and returned to duty.[6]

Florence Mew and Euselia Heape were gang-raped, yet they were repeatedly questioned if they had "resisted." One soldier was found guilty of the crime against the two women. Another was found guilty for aiding and abetting, and the rest were found guilty on lesser charges or set free.

Few details remain in the cases of Privates Alfred Catlett, Alexander Colwell, Charles Turner, and Washington Jackson. The men "stole out of camp ... and committed a brutal rape on the person of a young white woman after nearly killing her uncle and aunt, two very old people, who tried to prevent the outrage." The men were caught and tried by drumhead court-martial.[7] They were shot "before the whole regiment."[8]

Four men came to Sarah Hammond's house near Jacksonville, Florida. With a small child in her arms, she left to get provisions at camp. She walked about 200 yards before the men overtook her. Private Spencer Lloyd asked to hug her. Before she could respond, he embraced her, then took out his gun and threatened to shoot her. Sarah screamed. Lloyd said he would shoot her if she didn't stop. He threw her to the ground. She begged to return to her "babies." He warned her if she didn't lie still, he would kill her. With the child still in Sarah's arms, Lloyd raped her, then fled the scene.

Private John W. Cork tore the child from her arms. Another man held Sarah down, and Cork became the second soldier to rape her. After his assault, he watched while the other two men, John M. Smith and Wallace Baker, did the same. Captain T. D. Hodges came upon "four colored soldiers," then heard a woman scream. She was in a field and called for him.

"Those four men...," Sarah said, "downed me and did what they pleased to me, threatened me with their guns, said they'd shoot me if I made any noise, and that's mighty hard to take."

Hodges turned his horse around and galloped after the men. He kept them in sight until he met the quartermaster. Hodges had the quartermaster watch over the men while he reported the attack to the major. He got several men and Spencer, Cork, and Smith were arrested. Baker escaped. A drumhead court-martial was convened the same day. The Philadelphia *Press* reported that

> they were from the lowest strata of city life, and were among the hardest men in the regiment.... One of them had been pardoned for the commission of a crime for which he might have been shot.[9] During the last hour of life of these wretched men ... I found them sitting by a camp-fire with the guard, engaged in light ... conversation.... They read in my own uncontrollable emotions the message I had to convey. Being asked the question, "Are we convicted?" My silence imparted the

truth.... To the last they denied their crime amounted to a rape.

If there was any truth in their dying statements, the woman was *particeps criminis* [an accomplice]; but the evidence was overwhelming against them. All sense of shame and of chastity seemed to have been eradicated from their minds, and they were astonished that so much importance should be attached to so unimportant an affair. "Why were we not taught," they often repeated, "that such consequences would result from such an act?"... The hour of their execution arrived... and the cart stood ready to conduct them to the scaffold.... They took their seats and were carried to the place of execution.... The halters were then adjusted, and in about fifteen minutes all was over.... Cork and Lloyd were executed... near where the crime was committed... and Smith was taken to Jacksonville.... Their bodies still hang dangling in the air, and will not be removed till two o'clock to-day.

The *New York Herald* reported Smith's execution: "At twenty minutes' notice, a scaffold was erected, the troops called out, the citizens notified, and he had shared the righteous fate of his fellows. The body was allowed to remain twenty four hours before being cut down." The soldier who had escaped, Private Wallace Baker, was shot to death at a later date for "mutinous conduct."[10]

In Tennessee, Private Lawson Kemp of the 55th USCT Infantry had been reduced in rank from sergeant for drunkenness and neglect of duty. He was regarded as a "desperate villain" when he was caught swindling. Before charges could be brought, the captain of another company "got him out of prison and took him in his own company." Once there, Kemp "went foraging... when this felon ravished a white girl for which he was shot the next day." Kemp was tried by a drumhead court-martial, but the trial record no longer seems to exist.[11]

Little documentation remains regarding the case of Private Henry Jay of the 57th USCT. He was tried by a drumhead court-martial and executed the following day at Dardannell, Arkansas for the "rape on a white woman."[12]

All of the black men executed for the crime of rape notably raped white women. Due to lack of documentation, no serious analysis can be made of the cases of Privates Lawson Kemp and Henry Jay. Kemp had a previous history of making trouble and appears to have been drunk at the time of the assault. Such a history would have made a woman's word more believable in the eyes of a military court. With one exception, the remaining black soldiers executed all participated in gang rape and threatened the victims with weapons. Even then, not all of the men involved in the attacks received the death penalty.

The lone exception was Robert Henry Hughes. He had deserted and used an alias, a capital crime in itself. Although he did not commit rape, he attempted to rape an upper-class white woman. The fact that Johnson was black and had deserted would have made the woman's testimony completely believable at court-martial.

At least 275 Union soldiers were executed during the Civil War. Of those, 54.3 percent were black or foreign-born.[13] Eleven percent of the executions included rape or attempted rape convictions. Of the soldiers executed for sexual assaults, more than half were black. Instead of revealing "revenge rapes," as suggested by Reid Mitchell in *The Vacant Chair*, an analysis of the black men executed hints at racial bias. However, of the approximate 450 courts-martial for the crime of rape or attempted rape, almost 7 percent received the death sentence, revealing an even smaller proportion who were actually executed for a capital crime.

Chapter Five

"I Had Rather Die"

White Soldiers Who Received the Death Penalty

OUT OF THE NEARLY THIRTY UNION SOLDIERS executed for rape, twelve were white. In civilian cases, white men rarely received the death penalty. Only an examination of the records can reveal why these men suffered such a fate.

In Kansas, John Bell of the 2nd Kansas Cavalry was the first man to be legally executed. Celebrating Independence Day on July 4, 1862, he and another soldier got drunk. The two went to the home of Elisabeth Haywood and asked for water. She gave them a drink, and they left.

Before long, they returned, asking for something to eat. In the kitchen, she fixed supper. Bell did not eat, and his companion was so drunk that Bell said he was unable to ride his horse. With Elisabeth's help, he escorted his fellow soldier upstairs to sleep it off. Elisabeth returned to the kitchen. Bell followed her and closed the door behind them. She begged him to let her go. "He caught me and threw me down and ravished me." If she made any noise, he said that he would blow her brains out.

After the assault, Elisabeth woke up her "little boy," but Bell entered the room and raped her twice more in front of her son. When he finished, "he wanted his supper." She told him to go into the kitchen, and she sent her son to get help.

Back at camp, Bell admitted that "he had tryed to coax the woman to have intercourse with him. She refused." When he was unable to coax her, he bragged that he had thrown her to the floor and pulled up her clothes. Several witnesses identified Bell, and he was tried by a drum-head court-martial. Elisabeth's husband was a member of a neighboring regiment, the 9th Kansas Cavalry. Bell was found guilty and sentenced to hang. "Accordingly on Friday, the 11th, in the presence of the whole regiment, he was executed. He was a hardened wretch, and only got his just deserts."[1]

Decorated with medals for bravery in the British army during the Crimean War, Private Thomas R. Dawson left his post one night while on picket duty. Along with two other men, he came upon a house where they found alcohol and freely indulged. Dawson had no recollection as to what came later, but the other two men apparently got away.[2]

Frances West, nearly sixty years old, said that Dawson raised the latch of her door and walked in, speaking in "vulgar talk." He threw her on the bed and said he would do as he pleased. Frances managed to get away and ran to call the picket line. Dawson caught up with her, clapped his hand over her mouth, choked her, and pulled her back into the house. Once again, she escaped his grip, only to be overpowered outside the house and raped.

After the assault, he returned her to the house, threw her on the bed, and "swore he would continue to do as he pleased." He started to take off his clothes, and Frances saw her chance. This time she made it to the safety of the picket line and reported the attack.

Hearing a woman's screams, Corporal Hyde went to Frances's house and arrested Dawson. His suspenders, shoes, and cap were found, and "the bed was wet." Dawson "offered one of our men fifty dollars to shoot him and he said that he ought to be ashamed of himself—an old soldier—to be caught in such a scrape."

Dawson pleaded guilty to deserting his post and was found guilty of rape as well. He was sentenced to hang.[3] The 19th Massachusetts Volunteers submitted a petition to President Lincoln:

> Previous to the commission of a violent act for which he has been condemned, he was an excellent soldier, intelligent, and obedient. Since his trial, he has been . . . an inmate of the Regimental Hospital without a guard, and had every opportunity to effect his escape had he desired to do so. He served in the Crimean War . . . and obtained the Victoria Medal and Cross of Honor, bestowed only upon the bravest and most daring soldiers of that splendid force.

Chaplain William Corby personally delivered the petition to Lincoln. The president agreed to pardon Dawson if General Meade would as well. Meade replied that the president "should have given the final and positive decision. I will *not* act."[4]

On the day of Dawson's execution, he was placed in an open wagon and seated on his coffin. A band played the dead march.

> Dawson smiled and bowed to those he recognized. When he arrived at the scaffold... he ran up the steps, and... said, "Good-by, comrades... I thank you for what you have done for me. May you live long and die a happy death; I die an innocent man." ... Poor Dawson was launched into eternity, but not so soon as was intended; the rope was new and stretched so much that his feet touched the ground, and the provost marshal was obliged to take a turn in the rope... After he was pronounced dead by the surgeon he was taken down.... The troops marched past.
>
> The remarks were that it was too bad to hang men when they were so hard to get, and if they had let him alone a few weeks Johnnie Reb would have saved them the trouble.[5]

In spite of Dawson's proud declaration of innocence at his death, even he had admitted that he recalled nothing of the night at his court-martial. A woman's screams, Dawson's personal effects being left at the scene, and his attempted bribery of a guard speak more strongly to the likelihood of what happened on that April night in Virginia.

On March 12, 1864, Margaret Brooks traveled in her buggy from Memphis, Tennessee, to her home in Shelby County. George Bradshaw led the way in a wagon carrying goods. While crossing a stream, one of the lines on the mule team broke. Bradshaw unhitched the team and climbed aboard one of the mules to get help. Margaret and a Mr. Moore, who had accompanied her, checked on the wagon. When she crossed the stream, she heard "hooting and hollering." Three Union cavalrymen rode up and Moore scrambled away, leaving Margaret to fend for herself. The men threatened to shoot her if she didn't halt. Frightened, she hesitated before returning to the buggy. She attempted to turn the buggy around, but Irish-born Private John Callaghan told her not to move or "they would blow my brains into hell."

Privates Johnson and Snover, 2nd New Jersey Cavalry, went searching for Moore. Callaghan remained behind and asked Margaret for "Green Backs." A short while later the other men returned, and Callaghan stated that if Margaret had no money, "we want a little 'Fucking' and we intend to have it right here and the stiller you are about it the better it will be for you." Margaret claimed she would "die right here before I submit to any such thing."

Callaghan drew a gun and asked her if she would submit. She replied in the negative, and he said they would no longer ask. "We will do it any how." To keep her from screaming, he covered her mouth and choked her. The other men held her down while Callaghan raped her. In turn, he assisted the others as each took his turn raping her. Afterward, Callaghan said, " 'By God' you would not let me get through and I intend to have it over again." Callaghan raped her a second time, then searched her person and robbed her of $250. At the court martial, Margaret was asked if she resisted the men. "I did everything in my power."

Dr. F.T. Payne testified that Margaret had been "roughly handled." When asked about Margaret's chastity, he replied that it was "proper and without a stain." Private Michael Riley stated that Callaghan had said the three of them had a little "screwing" and were drunk on the day in question. The three men were sentenced to be shot by musketry.[6]

Private John Carroll of the 20th Wisconsin was charged with conduct prejudicial to good order and military discipline, assault with intent to commit rape, and assault with intent to kill. In Brownsville, Texas, armed with a musket, Carroll had gone to the home of Elisha Gidon. Outside the door, he ordered a light to be turned on and for the door to be opened. Gidon's wife, Mary, opened the door, and Carroll followed Gidon as he charged out the back door.

After firing his musket at Gidon, Carroll returned to the house, reloaded his gun, and set it down before placing his hands on Mary's shoulders. He commanded her to put her child down and lie on the bed. If she failed to hurry, he would shoot her. Thinking quickly, Mary stated that she would shut the door first. Instead of closing the door, she ran across the road to a neighbor's house, saving herself from being raped. Carroll continued his rampage by terrorizing the neighbors. Before the night was over, the neighbor, Mrs. Flores, lay wounded. In his defense, Carroll admitted that he had been drunk. He was found guilty on all charges and sentenced to be shot by musketry. Closer inspection of Carroll's record reveals that he had a history of arrests. He was executed on November 11, 1864.[7]

In June 1864, Irish-born Sergeant Charles Sperry ordered two privates, John Martin and John Tully, to accompany him to the house of

James Nelson in Fairfax County, Virginia, in search of "rebels." Upon reaching their destination, they knocked on the door and pulled Nelson outside, leaving Tully to guard him. The two remaining soldiers searched the house looking for enemy soldiers.

Fifteen-year-old Annie Nelson joined her mother Sarah in her bedroom. She heard the men searching upstairs. Sperry returned to the first floor and entered the bedroom, grabbing Annie's arm. She gave this account:

> Mother came to the door. He ... pointed the pistol at Mother and let go of my arm. I went towards the door and ... he grabbed hold me again and pushed me up against the wall and struck me twice with his fist. I tried to get away from him. He struck me on the head with the pistol. ... I was screaming. He said if I did not hush my noise there was twenty outside and they would come in and kill me. He said his orders were to ... kill me anyhow. He said I had to surrender to him. I told him I would die before I would. He struck me twice more with the pistol. He attempted to put his hands under my clothes.

Martin entered the room, lending Annie the chance to escape and hide. Martin was found guilty of forcibly breaking and entering the Nelson house and aiding and assisting Sperry to commit rape. He received three months at hard labor, and Tully was acquitted. Sperry was charged with quitting his guard without urgent necessity or leave, drunkenness on duty, assault and battery with intent to commit rape, and rape. He stated, "I do not recollect of taking any improper freedom with the girl." With a prior history of desertion in 1863, he was found guilty on all charges except rape. He was executed in March 1865.[8]

On the night of June 18, 1864, Privates Daniel Geary and Ransom Gordon went to the house of Mary Stiles in Prince George County, Virginia. Both men had stopped by earlier in the day with other men, but Geary and Gordon returned that evening with sugar and coffee. Upon arrival, they asked Mary if she could make some coffee, which she did with the help of her forty-eight-year-old cousin Lucy Williams.

Mary informed Gordon that her "husband was a Union man." To put her mind at ease, Gordon said that he and Geary would guard her if she would place a mattress on the floor in the hall. Though afraid, she did as he asked, went to the room she shared with her two small children and cousin, and locked the door behind her.

Later in the night, the men woke Mary by asking for some water. Her cousin handed the pitcher out the door, but Gordon set it down. He grabbed Mary's arm and demanded that she accompany him. Struggling to get away, she refused. She screamed, and the men assured her they would not hurt her. Geary then seized her, and they carried her into the hall.

Near the mattress on the floor, they suggested what they wanted, and she replied, "I had rather die." Geary held her down while Gordon raped her. Then they traded places.

Like civilian cases, during the court-martial, the defense asked Mary whether she had resisted and why she had allowed them to "do it." After being raped by the two men, Mary stated she had returned to her room and locked the door. A short time later, Gordon and Geary left and she got her children and cousin together, taking them into the woods. When daylight arrived, she went to her mother's and relayed what had happened.

Cousin Lucy testified and corroborated Mary's account. Afraid for her own life, she had remained in the room with the children. When Mary returned to the room she was crying and said, "I had rather he would have shot me."

Two witnesses for Gordon, Private Horace Cox and Sergeant Charles Ludlow, claimed that Gordon had said that Mary "would let him diddle her for the coffee and sugar." Gordon made the statement that Mary went willingly. "She laid down herself and permitted us to gratify ourselves."

The defense introduced Geary as a witness for Gordon. At first, the Judge Advocate objected, but after deliberation, it was agreed to allow Geary to testify on Gordon's behalf. He testified that Mary went willingly and gave no resistance. He claimed that Gordon had said in advance that she was "going to let him have some fucking." Both Gordon and Geary were found guilty and sentenced to hang in July 1864.[9]

One author claimed that Mary "confessed on her deathbed years after the war that she 'swore the lives of these men away in order to contribute her mite toward the extermination of the Yankee army.' "[10] No citation is given for the allegation. Even if Mary had initially stated that her husband was a Union man out of fear, in the hope the men would not plunder her house, crying rape rarely produced a death sentence, especially for white men.

The Philadelphia *Press* reported:

With tears in her eyes, she sought an audience with Gen. M. R.

General M. R. Patrick and staff

Patrick.... [He] listened to her touching story, and promised to do all in his power to assist in bringing the criminals to light, at the same time informing her that it would be almost next to an impossibility to find the guilty ones among an army numbering over one hundred thousand men. By a singular circumstance the perpetrators were discovered. Unable to keep the secret of their fiendish conduct to themselves, they boasted of their feat among the men of their company and regiment.[11]

Provost Marshal General M. R. Patrick wrote in his diary about Gordon:

There seemed to be no clew [sic] to the perpetrators, at first, but the leader could not keep away from the Spot, after the crime, & was the *first* to speak of it— He was arrested & to make his own Story good, he had to tell of his comrade— They were identified by the woman & her cousin.

On July 15, he continued:

> They mounted the Scaffold & there I read the Order of the
> Court & Sentence— The Clergy talked with them. . . . they died
> hoping for the mercy thro' Jesus Christ & acknowledging the
> justice of the Sentence about to be executed—[12]

A priest who had consulted with Geary before the execution stated in his
memoirs, "The crime was much, if not entirely, the fault of his accomplice
rather than his own."[13]

The *Press* agreed:

> The character of Gordon was vicious, and he was recognized
> in his regiment as a man of brutality. At one time he repre-
> sented himself as a safety guard in the house of a Mr. Thomas
> Jones. . . . When Mr. Jones was asleep, Gordon arose and stole
> everything of any value from the house, and left for parts un-
> known. He afterwards came to his regiment, but nothing was
> complained of his conduct.[14]

However, Geary had been no stranger to trouble and had deserted on at
least three occasions.[15] Gordon and Geary were hanged on July 15, 1864.
An Ohio paper reported the details:

> Gordon was a very large man. . . . Geary was a smaller per-
> son. . . . Before the condemned mounted the steps their hands
> had been securely tied behind them. All the persons upon the
> platform descended, save one who, with dispatch proceeded to
> adjust the ropes around their necks and tied their feet. . . . He
> took a piece of white napkin several feet long and wrapped it
> around their heads, leaving a small aperture for breathing. The
> eyes of the multitude closed as the sound of the drum signaled
> the falling trap.
>
> The men hung thirty-five minutes. After witnessing this
> feast of death, the vast crowd dispersed.[16]

Provost General Patrick went to see Mary Stiles in September following
the execution. "I did not go in, but seeing Mrs. Stiles near the fence, rode
up and asked of their welfare. She said they were very little molested, as
they have a Safe Guard—and she is now 'All Right'."[17] The statement that
Mary confessed to the men's innocence on her deathbed appears to be
an unsubstantiated rumor.

In North Carolina, Private James Preble drank whiskey before going to a home where three women lived. As a distraction, Letitia Craft, fifty-eight years old, had given her nieces Louisa Jane Bedard and Rebecca Drake some chores to tend to. Preble followed the women inside and began bothering the younger ones with vulgar expressions that he intended "criminal connections" with them. He threw his arm around Louisa's waist and unbuttoned his pants. When he attempted to throw her down on a chest, she slipped away and bolted out of the house. Turning his attention to the other woman, Preble tried to grab Rebecca. He exposed himself and strutted around with a pistol in his hand.

Letitia stated, "I thought that I being an old woman that no man or no thing, for I do not call such a thing a man, would bother me, so I told them [her nieces] to run." The women escaped to the barn area, but Preble went after them. The women hid behind the "fodder stacks" and watched him shoot the family's cow. Unable to find the women, Preble grew further agitated and returned to the house, threatening Letitia that if she failed to tell him where the women were, he would kill her. He dragged her into the bedroom and ordered her onto the bed.

"I told him I shouldn't and begged just as hard as ever a person could beg, but the more I begged the worse he acted and he then threw me down on the bed and gave me my ruin. . . . I tried to 'holler.' "

Preble responded, "You damned old secesh bitch if you do not hush hallowing [hollering] I will kill you." To keep Letitia from screaming, Preble placed his arm over her mouth, then raped her.

After receiving word that one of the men was drunk, Sergeant Arthur Wood rode to the residence, looking for Preble. He relayed his experience:

> I . . . rapped at the door but got no answer though I heard groaning inside. I then went to the back-door and found it open. I went inside and saw a woman coming out of the bedroom crying. I asked her what was the matter, but got no answer. I saw blood all over her and blood on the floor. . . . I asked her if she was shot. She said no that she was raped.

Letitia pointed to the bedroom. Wood found Preble lying on the bed with his pants unbuttoned and a pistol in his hand. His pants and shirt were covered in blood. When questioned what he was doing there, Preble merely laughed. Wood confiscated the private's gun and shoved him outside. Private James Hogan had remained outside with the horses. Preble came out of the house with "his privates hanging out of his pants" and laughing. Through the half-open door, Hogan saw an old woman crying. As Preble mounted his horse, he remarked that "he had done more work than the whole battalion had that day." For his escapades, Preble was found guilty of assault with intent to commit rape on Rebecca Drake and Louisa Bedard and of raping Letitia Craft. He was sentenced to be shot with musketry.

On March 31, 1865, by the order of General Sherman, Preble was escorted to the tune of the "Dead March" before the firing squad. An officer had been chosen to load a dozen rifles with powder and ball, except for one, which was loaded with powder only. "He then mixed the guns so thoroughly that he himself could scarcely tell which guns were loaded with ball and which one was not." Preble was placed in front of his coffin and shot. Afterward the remaining men marched past his dead body.[18]

Twice-widowed Martha Simpson was riding her mare home in Montgomery County, Arkansas, when Irish-born Private John Vincent of the 3rd U.S. Cavalry met her on the "highway." He asked her a few questions, including where the next house was before grabbing her mare's bridle and leading her from the road. Once out of sight from passersby, he told her to dismount the mare. She screamed, and he pulled her from the mare's back. To keep her from screaming further, Martha said, "He clamped his hand on my mouth and threw me down on the ground. He told me what he was going to do in as rough a way as he could and he went at it with all his desire."

During Vincent's court-martial, Martha was severely questioned about what parts of his body were exposed and if she felt his bare body. She responded, "I felt his stomach on mine and his breast struck against mine. He was between my legs and I felt his legs against mine. He had his member in me clear up to the body."

The usual resistance questions were asked. Martha satisfied them by saying she had tried to push Vincent off and screamed. Then she was asked, "How long did the accused remain on you?"

"Until he satisfied his passion," Martha answered.

The Judge Advocate asked, "How do you know?"

"I have been married long enough to remember he had satisfied his passion."

Then she was asked to clarify her response on what Vincent had said he was going to do to her in a "rough way."

"He said he would fuck me and he did so."

The defense attempted to discredit Martha as a witness by asking how she could have been raped if Vincent had kept a hand over her mouth the entire time. Martha responded that he was much stronger than she. Vincent's statement to the court used the same line of reasoning:

> I must be an unusual strong man or that she was a very willing victim to the crime charged.... a Rape could not have been committed in the way the witness stated.
>
> Mrs. Simpson swears that I held my hand over her mouth from the time she was dragged from the horse to the time I should have left her; that I, having one hand always occupied, with the other one threw her down... threw up her clothes, parted her legs and committed all the acts.... I think the court will easy [sic] see, that this is impossible—without her consent.

The court did not believe Vincent. He was found guilty of rape and desertion and sentenced to hang.[19]

With the exception of Sergeant Charles Sperry, all of the white men who received death sentences were privates. Of the twelve soldiers who were executed for the crime of rape, eight had been drinking alcohol. Seven cases involved the use of weapons. All were guns. Eight soldiers were guilty of other crimes ranging from robbery to assault with intent to kill.

Privates Dawson, Callaghan, and Vincent and Sergeant Sperry were foreign-born soldiers. Like black soldiers, they were discriminated against more often. Even though they made up approximately 26 percent of the white Union soldiers, the number of foreign-born men executed was 28 percent higher than the average.[20] Even then, Sperry was found not guilty of rape.

Four white soldiers remain who were executed for the crime of rape alone. Private John Bell raped the wife of a fellow Union cavalry member; both he and Private James Preble had been drinking. Preble had attempted to rape three women and succeeded in raping one. These women had male witnesses to corroborate their testimony.

The remaining two soldiers executed for the crime of rape alone, Privates Gordon and Geary, had a long history of military trouble making, including desertion, which served to make the woman's testimony more believable.

Many period sources state that men who raped deserved death. The reality was clearly very different. Women had to prove they had been raped, and white men rarely received such a punishment.

Alexandria, Virginia, Slave Pen — Union military prison

Chapter Six

"I Did Not Give My Consent"

Black Victims

THE ARGUMENT THAT THE CIVIL WAR was a low-rape war usually ignores the fact that black women were rarely taken seriously when they were raped.

In December 1864, Union Brigadier Saxton reported to Secretary of War Stanton:

> The women were held as the legitimate prey of lust, and as they had been taught it was a crime to resist a white man they had not learned to dare to defend their chastity. Licentiousness was widespread; the morals of the old plantation life seemed revived in the army of occupation.[1]

A chaplain gave his first sermon on the upper deck of a boat. The crew went ashore for some wood, and his preaching became very difficult among disordered confusion. About a hundred soldiers immediately went ashore "shouting and singing . . . into the woods to have a little recreation." One man shot a dog and another caught a calf. The chaplain wrote in his diary: "Still another soldier stepped up to a colored lady, who had come out of her cabin, and, grasping her round the waiste [sic], forcibly marched off with her under his arm, while she struggled to get loose, and a hundred voices cheered." Instead, of going to the woman's (or the dog's or calf's) aid, the chaplain was afraid to look around for fear of losing his "discourse, and thus render my first sermon a failure."[2]

Newspapers occasionally reported the rape of black women. One correspondent went into great detail about the specific acts of arson, pillaging, and plundering that took place near Fredericksburg, Virginia, almost a year after the battle of the same name. He also stated that he had heard "of a well vouched case of rape upon the person of a negro child eleven years old." Also in Virginia, General Butler's force (New Orleans fame) burned houses and "ravished a negro woman, besides committing other outrages of a similar fiendish nature."[3]

A Massachusetts officer was involved in another report when he "attempted to outrage a colored woman in [the] presence of her husband, after having offered a large sum of money to gain their consent, and failing, threatened to shoot the husband if he interfered, and finally maltreated the guard who came to the rescue."[4]

In a couple of instances, soldiers and citizens fought back to protect their wives and loved ones. In Tennessee, two soldiers were found bruised and stabbed to death and a third was severely injured. The reason was believed to be a result of "insults offered to colored women" after the three men had gone to the home of a black soldier. The house had two doors; two of the soldiers guarded the doors while the third went inside. He "attempted to ravish the wife of the colored soldier, who was at that time in bed." The husband's gun failed to discharge. "He then used it as a club and thus by slaying the attempted ravishers, rescued his wife."[5]

In a similar situation, three drunken sailors visited a contraband camp. One "entered a house in which there was a female, who seems to have been the principle object of attraction," while his companions waited outside. A party of black men gathered outside and ran two of the sailors off. But the third was shot to death.[6]

When newspapers reported the rapes of black women, the women were generally not named. The assaults were often mentioned in passing, when husbands retaliated to protect their wives or if white witnesses were present. Otherwise, the sexual assaults of black women were not considered newsworthy.

During August 1863, Private Patrick Tully of the 12th New York Cavalry went to Sampson Dennis's home in North Carolina. He claimed he was officer of the night and looking for a missing man. Shortly after, he informed Dennis he would be staying the night. Dennis, an elderly black man, denied Tully's request and sent Casey Ransom, a woman who was staying in his household, after the guards to evict the private. By the time Casey returned with the guards, Tully had gone into hiding. Worried that

Tully would return, Dennis conveyed his fears to the guards. The guard told him to "shut the door and lay down," and left.

Barely was Casey "lying on her pallet" and Dennis "in my bed," when someone rapped on the window. Tully's voice came from outside the door, threatening to shoot if it wasn't opened. Dennis cracked the door and heard a pistol cock. Tully forced his way inside and began looking for Casey. He found her hiding under the bed and pulled her out. "He began to handle her very rough." Dennis attempted to get the woman out of the house. After a short scuffle with Tully, he found himself locked out of his own house. He peered through a crack by the door "and could see them plain. There was a great fire in the fire place. They tussled around. He have her down and I saw him when he got on her. I then ran after the guard as fast as I could."

Inside the house, Tully offered Casey a two-dollar bill. She refused the money and he threatened to hit her on the side of her head with his pistol if she screamed. Casey stated: "This man [Tully] threw me down on the floor.... He did not let me up.... He pulled up my clothes. He took his 'what's his name' out and tried to put it into me. He did put it into me. I did not like it." During Tully's court-martial, Casey was asked to clarify what Tully had put into her. To this she responded, "his pecker." Again, she was asked to clarify. "The thing he calls his prick."

A standard resistance question was asked. Casey said, "I tried my best to get away from him. He was stronger than I was, and had a pistol in his hand." The court then wanted clarification as to where Tully had put his "prick."

"He put it in my cunt," Casey replied. The court was finally satisfied of which body parts had gone where.

During this era, a defendant was allowed to cross-examine an accuser, and Tully proceeded with Casey. He inquired if she had commenced their interaction on the night in question by asking him to sit down and share some whiskey with her. Casey denied the accusation. In Tully's statement to the court, he claimed nothing had happened that night. He was found guilty and given two years, hard labor and a dishonorable discharge. He died from tuberculosis before serving his full sentence.[7]

In Louisiana, Corporal William Hilton of the 16th Indiana got drunk and began harassing the "negroes" on the Pelton plantation. He rode up to a "half-grown" (her age was not given) girl by the name of Julia and asked her "if she was a friend to the yankees."

"Yes sir," Julia replied.

Hilton commanded that she hold his horse. The girl grew frightened and started crying. He demanded that she stop or he would shoot her. When Hilton fired at the girl, Nancy Simpson, a "colored" citizen, came to Julia's aid. The shot missed Julia, but he put his hand on her, then turned to Nancy and asked if she was "a Union lady." Nancy confirmed that she was, but Hilton had his pants down. Nancy begged him to leave Julia alone:

> He threw her down on the ground and tried to ravish her. He said he wanted to ride her. I tried to get her away, and told him to let her alone, that she was not big enough, and that there were plenty other women, but he said no, he wanted that little yellow girl, and that if she did not let him ride her, he would shoot her.

Hilton placed his pistol to Julia's head, near "the temple and shot her brains out." He was charged with attempt to commit rape and murder. He was found guilty on both charges and sentenced to hang. The sentence was never carried out. An irregularity was discovered in his court-martial. In the documentation, Hilton was listed as a private, not a corporal, which was a "gross irregularity." Non-commissioned officers were to be reduced in rank before "corporeal punishment."

William Hilton escaped the guardhouse while awaiting his court-martial but was merely reduced in rank to a private for attempt of rape and the murder of a "mulatto girl and returned to duty."[8]

Jennie Green, a girl of unknown age, had escaped slavery. Under the wing of Chaplain William Hunter, she had found freedom among the Yankees. When the cavalry came to City Point, Virginia, they had wounded that needed tending. Hunter helped unload ambulances while a couple of men asked Nellie Wyatt and Jennie Green to cook for them.

The room the women entered had no wood or fireplace for cooking. Nellie was told that she would be left alone because she was married. Lieutenant Andrew Smith caught Jennie's coat sleeve, pulled her into another room, and locked the door. He threw her on the floor. Jennie recounted what happened next:

> I told him to let me alone. He said he was not going to let me alone. He unbuttoned his own breeches. He hurt me. I tried to pull away. He said if I did not stop ... he was going to kill me. When I was lying on the floor he layed down too. He ... put something against me—not his hand—that was what hurt

me. He did the same thing that married people do.... I did not give my consent. I was trying... to get away from him, I hollowed and tried to pull away.... I was lying on my back, and the man was lying on my belly. I crossed my feet, he took hold of them... and pulled them apart, the[n] he laid down on my belly, and... I felt the pain... he put something into me.... He stayed on me till somebody came and knocked at the door.

Jennie's testimony reads very much like that of a young girl or adolescent.

While Jennie was locked in the room with Smith, Nellie had gone for help. By the time she returned with Chaplain Hunter, Jennie's screams were coming from behind the door. Hunter called outside the door. When no response came, he forced the door open. A man rushed out of the room, and Jennie was on the floor crying. She told the chaplain what had happened.

When Smith burst out of the room, Lieutenant C.A. Bennet told him to halt. Smith paid no attention, and Bennet followed him to Colonel Spears's quarters. Lieutenant Smith was in the room with the colonel. Instead of confronting the situation, Bennet reported the incident to the provost marshal. During Smith's court-martial, Bennet specifically noted that with all of the activity of unloading wounded and the noise around him, a girl's screams could have gone unheard.

Also during the court-martial, Colonel Spears, a lieutenant colonel, three majors, and a captain were called to testify on the behalf of Smith's character. All reported that he was an excellent officer and gentleman, with one exception. One major had known Smith since he was a boy and stated that Smith's good character had the exception of "drinking too much."

In spite of Smith's character witnesses, he was found guilty of conduct unbecoming an officer and gentleman and rape. He was dismissed from the service and sentenced to ten years at hard labor.[9] Ironically, General Butler, who had threatened the women of New Orleans with rape as a war tactic, agreed with the sentence. In fact, he noted that it had been "a day or two since a negro man was hung, in the presence of the army, for the attempted violation of the person of a white woman. Equal and exact justice would have taken this officer's life."[10]

Smith's regiment sent pleas on his behalf to President Lincoln for clemency. Other letters were sent Lincoln's way asking for the same.

Smith's attorney, William Johnston, wrote a lengthy letter stating that a young woman had been caught in "an act of shame and pretended to be ravished." He excused Smith's excess drinking as "a frailty too often found in noble natures." Because of Smith's good character he was incapable of such crime, if he had been sober. "If he was intoxicated it may account for an act of indecency, very reprehensible but falling far short of a rape upon a child." He added, "If Jennie was a young child ravished by a full grown man both her person and garments would have exhibited unmistakable signs of violence." Only Nellie had heard Jennie's cries, when the house had been "filled from bottom to top" with soldiers who would have come to her aid. Therefore "silence gives consent." No one saw Jennie being abused, except that she was "whimpering," which any person would do if caught in the "act of fornication." A woman who truly guards her chastity would give "wild, piercing and terrific shrieks."

The fact that Jennie's life had been threatened verbally meant nothing to Johnston—it would have taken a deadly weapon to subdue a chaste woman from *allowing* herself to be raped. He went on to state that someone (not Smith) had gone into the room with Jennie

> by mutual consent for the purpose of sinful amusement, and being surprised and exposed, as a thousand other women have done she pretended she was ravished when she was caught in a act of shame. Every lawyer who has had experience in the criminal courts knows that nine-tenths of all rapes and attempts to commit rape in the world are fictitious. A wicked woman who fails in her attempt to seduce a man... pretends that an attempt was made to ravish her. A weak woman who is caught in the fact covers her shame by the pretense.... Men have gone to parts unknown in order that the victims of their lust might take the benefit of the pretense.

Furthermore, a court-martial was not the place to try morals, but "offences against our country." A rape trial should only be held by jury, and no jury would have found Smith guilty.[11]

After receiving the letters attesting to Smith's excellent character, President Lincoln pardoned him. He wrote to the Secretary of War Edwin M. Stanton:

> Gen. Butler, Mr. Holt, and yourself, each in turn, on examination of the evidence thought there was no doubt of his guilt, while I thought there was some slight room for doubt.... I concluded to let him suffer for a while, and then discharge him.

Twice within two or three weeks I made short order for his pardon for the unexecuted part of the sentence, which, however it seems has not yet been done. Let it be done now.[12]

Traveling by cart, Laura Ennis was on her way home in Virginia with James Carey. Armed with guns and an ax, Privates Charles Clark and Joseph Redmond halted the cart and asked for some change. Neither party had any money to make change.

Clark ordered Laura to "get out of the Cart." When she explained she was unable, he jumped into the cart and shoved her. Laura said that she was "very poorly and sick." The two privates struggled with Laura. She caught hold of Carey to keep from being forced out, but the men overpowered her. Redmond dragged Laura into the woods while Clark kept guard over Carey. Although the court-martial record was not explicit, it suggested that Redmond raped Laura in the woods.

When Redmond finished, he guarded Carey, and Clark entered the woods. After Redmond's attack, Laura had difficulty getting up and was on her hands and knees. She said:

He [Clark] met Redmond as he was coming out of the woods. I begged him to let me alone and cried. He said if I made any noise he would stuff my mouth with anything he could get hold of; he then Ravished me. After he was done with me he got up and went into the road.... He told [me], that if I reported him ... he would shoot me, hang me to a tree and would skin me.

Clark was found guilty of rape and threats to shoot Laura if she reported the rape. He was sentenced to forfeit all pay and five years, hard labor. However, the prison where he supposedly served his sentence reported no record of his case. Redmond deserted in March 1865 and apparently was never found for either charge.[13]

In South Carolina, Privates Albert Opedyke and Samuel Miller of the 38th Ohio were awakened by the screams of an unidentified woman of "African descent." Private Thomas Killgore was in the process of raping the woman while four men held her down. Afterward, Killgore said to Private David Kunkle that he could "screw her." Because of the woman's kicking and screaming, Kunkle was unsuccessful in his attempt.

"Then, he [Killgore] said he wanted to see what she had for a 'thing.' " Opedyke described what happened next: "Then Kilgore took the torch, put his right foot on her right leg, caught her by her dress with his left hand, pulled up her clothes and threw the torch in between her legs and burnt her." Even though the woman was tortured, the court asked the witnesses the standard resistance questions.

In spite of two white male eyewitnesses, there was no *proof* of penetration. Killgore was only found guilty of assault with intent to commit rape. He was sentenced to ten years, hard labor and Kunkle received four years.[14] The victim never testified, nor was she identified. Neither were the other three men involved. Why the men who had witnessed the crime never came to the woman's aid was also never mentioned.

Assistant Surgeon Charles F. Lauer of the 55th Pennsylvania was charged with numerous assaults on the slaves and the children of the foreman at the Milne plantation in North Carolina. His court-martial began with Lauer refusing to plead to the charges of assault with attempt to commit rape, conduct prejudicial to good order and military discipline, and conduct unbecoming an officer and a gentleman. He claimed, "They include such a length of time as to prevent the possibility of either disproving them; or defending himself against them; and he therefore hopes the Court will not entertain them."

The court refused Lauer's request. He continued his protest until the court stated that "the acts are charged against an ignorant set of people who cannot *with very great accuracy* state at what *dates* the acts were committed but who can state *within what limits* they took place." When the first witness, a slave, was called, Lauer objected once more "until it be made clear that she understands the nature of an oath and whether the one she is about to take will be binding on her conscience." Rebecca Smith was declared competent by the court and relayed her story.

Near the house, she sat on a bench with three boys who waited on officers. Lauer came along and sat beside her. He asked her to "do it." When she refused, Lauer followed her to her house and asked her again. Unable to accept refusal, he slapped and beat Laura. She called for help and "the Doctor took a chair and struck me over the eye."

Rebecca reported the incident to Captain Nesbit, who said "he did not think the Doctor would do such a thing." During the court-martial, Rebecca showed where she had been hit by the chair.

Lauer cross-examined Rebecca himself and asked her, "Did you fall over a chair and cut your face?" Rebecca replied in the negative, and he asked, "Did you fall against the door and cut your face?" Abusers frequently attempt to blame the victim.

When Eda, another slave, was called as a witness, Lauer once again objected on the grounds she did not understand the meaning of an oath. Eda was declared a competent witness. Lauer had come to her house she said, to "knock me." He struck her with his fist and threatened her. "He came into my house and fought with me, and I had to go into the cotton fields to sleep for three nights to keep away from him."

At the home of Susan Jackson, Lauer broke down the door with an ax. He then went to Sarah Jackson's door and broke it open the same way. He dragged Sarah out of the room by her neck. He beat Sarah and said, "if that girl did not give up to him he would Kill her sure." Lauer cross-examined Susan, "Did Sarah Jackson say . . . Northern women were all bad women or all whores?" Susan replied in the negative.

Rumors had spread among the soldiers that a slave by the name of Jane Taylor had given a number of soldiers in the regiment venereal disease. Accompanied by two officers, Lauer examined Jane. "Two of them and the Doctor took hold of me and threw me down over the table. They raised my clothes as high as my waist and searched me." He exposed her to one of the other officers. Captain S.S. Metzger, one of the officers present, admitted Lauer had failed to use "propriety." He went on to state that Jane's reputation for chastity was "very hard indeed." He repeated the answer when asked about Jane's morality and veracity. In fact, the character of all the "Negro population" at the Milne plantation "was very hard indeed." When asked what he meant by the statement, he replied, "The majority of them were prostitutes."

Several other officers were called during the court-martial, ranging in rank from lieutenant to colonel. All commended Lauer as having a good reputation as an officer and a gentlemen. Most of them stated the women involved had bad reputations, all reporting on hearsay. Lieutenant Parsons even resorted to the use of the word in his testimony: "I do not know much about them. But from hearsay, and seeing them around, I think it is bad."

For his repeated sexual abuse, Lauer was found guilty of assault with attempt to commit rape against Rebecca and examining Jane. Because he had been under orders, the examination charge and all other charges were dismissed. For the single guilty charge, Lauer was sentenced to have his pay suspended for two months and to be publicly reprimanded.[15]

Mary Budget approached Captain A. W. Thompson of the 115th Ohio Infantry. Her "privates" were "bleeding profusely and appeared to be badly torn." She told the captain that the "deed had been committed by soldiers." A doctor examined her, and Private Frederick Cox was charged with assault and battery with intent to commit rape and being absent without leave. Cox admitted to "being with Mary." A short court-martial followed. Besides the captain, three men testified, revealing little except to place doubt on Mary's chastity because "she had the Pox," and she had been injured due to "intemperance." Mary was never called to testify, and Cox was to forfeit his pay for two months. The sentence was disapproved and he was returned to duty.[16]

Near Winchester, Virginia, Corporal George Hakes went to the home of Cornelius Robinson. He sat by the fire and asked Robinson if he would get a sheepskin from the neighboring widow. If Robinson was willing, Hakes said he would pay him well for it.

After Robinson left, Hakes asked Robinson's wife, Phoebe if she had any "rebels in the house," to which she replied that she did not. Hakes got up, inspected the bedroom, and began asking questions about who slept where.

At that point, he grabbed Phoebe and said that if "I did not give up to him he would shoot me." She told him to shoot her. He said her "man was gone and he would do as he pleased." He threw her on the bed and drew his pistol. When she stated that "I would not give up to him," he threatened her again. Phoebe screamed to her little boy to get his father. Hakes pulled up her clothes, and "he put his privates in me. I resisted him—as long as . . . I could. I was not in good health." Phoebe had given birth less than three weeks before.

As Robinson approached the widow's house, where he was to get the sheepskin for Hakes, his son came running after him. He was crying and said that Hakes was after his mother. Robinson charged back to the house. Upon Robinson's arrival, Hakes rode off in a hurry. In the middle of the floor, Phoebe wept with blood running out of her mouth. She said, "The nasty man has done what he wanted with me and gone." Robinson went after Hakes and reported the crime to an officer on the nearby picket line.

Several puzzling aspects took place during Hakes's court-martial. Even though the trial surrounded the accusation that Hakes "did ravish the wife of one Cornelius Robinson," the actual charge against him was "conduct prejudicial to good order and military discipline," not rape.

Hakes cross-examined the victim severely. He asked Phoebe why she did not simply leave the room "when he first made advances to you?" along with the standard resistance questions. After those inquiries, the questioning got more personal. "When he gained entrance did you not try to throw him off?" "How long was he on you before he finished?" "Did he have an emission while having connection with you?" "Was the sensation pleasant or otherwise to you?" and "Have you had sexual intercourse with your husband since the birth of your child previous to this date?"

At no point did the Judge Advocate overrule Hakes's out-of-line questioning, and the victim was forced to relive the rape by her rapist yet again in front of the officers sitting on the court. In Hakes's final statement to the court, he was contradictory, claiming that his case was one of misidentification even though he had admitted to the captain of the 6th Michigan Cavalry that he had gone to the house to warm himself. He discussed the legal definition of rape at great length, then said:

> [Phoebe] does not show that she resisted the union to that extent that she might have done, nor that he used that amount of force that would have been necessary to make up the crime of rape. There was but a partial resistance on her part, as we all know that had she exerted herself to her utmost she might have prevented him from accomplishing his purpose in so short a time, as her husband was not gone over two minutes from the house.
>
> I shall therefore insist, that the woman ... wasn't ravished, but that, at first resisting afterwards submitted, and that there was fornication or adultery ... but that the force used was not sufficient to characterize the offense as the crime of Rape.

According to Hakes's statement, his character witnesses had proven he was a good soldier with a wife and child at home. The defense insisted he would not behave in such a manner.

The court pointed out the contradictions in Hakes's statement and gave him a dishonorable discharge and two years, hard labor. He was released after serving approximately a year.[17] While the case is noteworthy that a black woman's testimony was believed against a white man with contradictory testimony, it remains unclear why the charge against Hakes failed to include rape.

At the Point Lookout Small Pox Hospital in Maryland, John Hall of the 5th New Hampshire was seen leaving the tent of Mary Campbell. A patient herself, Mary reported to the assistant surgeon that "one of his men had been committing violence on her." She identified Hall and the surgeon placed him under arrest.

While the surgeon failed to examine Mary for signs of having been raped, he testified at Hall's court-martial that her manner gave the appearance she had been. "Her whole manner, her excited state, her sobs... She was in a state of great excitement." Private Jarvis Moore of the 36th USCT overheard Hall tell Mary "not to say anything to the Doctor or any of the rest about it." Three Confederate prisoners had identified Hall, but only one remained at the hospital at the time of the court-martial to present testimony. More than six months had passed from the time of the assault to Hall's court-martial. By that time, Mary could not be located to testify. As a result, Hall was found guilty of leaving his post, not rape. He was sentenced to three months at hard labor and the loss of pay for eight months.[18]

Ten-year-old America Pierman was gathering wood when Private Thomas Mitchell of the 1st New York Engineers approached her and said there were two gray jackets that she could have for her brother if she accompanied him to the "old camp." When they got to the camp, he caught her hand and pulled her into one of the huts. He made her lie down.

She said, "I begged him to let me go back to my mother. I called him master and said please let me go back home."

"God damn you hush," Mitchell responded. More than once, he threatened America's life. America continued: "He pulled my clothes up and touched me with his hands first. He hurt me after he laid down on me... I was bleeding real hard. He unbuttoned his pantaloons and took his things out after he had me lay down. I saw him—and exposed his person."

America sobbed the story to her father, who promptly reported the attack to Brevet General James Hall. When Hall questioned Mitchell on "why he had treated the little negro girl so," the private replied, "she wasn't a negro." Afterward, he stated he "didn't know anything about any girl." The general promptly placed Mitchell under arrest.

Surgeon Robert Loughram examined America. Her "hymen had been ruptured" and she had been bruised "near the entrance of the vagina." In his professional opinion, "rape committed upon the person of a child that age would produce" her injuries. Because America was a child, she wasn't subjected to any resistance questions, but she endured being cross-examined by her attacker. Mitchell was sentenced to a mere three years, hard labor and a dishonorable discharge for the rape of a ten-year-old girl.[19]

In Tennessee, three drunken soldiers from the 33rd Indiana Infantry rode their mules to the McKinley plantation. Private Perry Pierson approached Harriet and Matilda McKinley and asked Harriet if she was a slave. When she responded that she was, he told her that if she got on behind him she "would be a slave no longer." When she refused his offer, he tried to pull her onto the mule. The mule stepped on them, but Harriet and Matilda ran.

Pierson got off the mule and caught Harriet by the waist. She struggled and "Aunt Leah" got hold of his hand. With the other woman's aid, Harriet escaped and bolted for the house. Once inside, she sought refuge with Matilda. They locked the door and hid under a bed. The men searched the house and finally arrived at the room where the women were hiding. One man knocked and a voice told them if they didn't open the door, they would "come in, and kick hell out of us." Fearing for her life, Harriet told Matilda to open the door. Harriet jumped out the window, but Pierson followed her. Eventually, he caught her. She kicked and screamed as he dragged her to the smokehouse. There, he "flung his knees in my back" and threw her on the ground. "He got on top of me, and held me down; he pulled up my clothes."

In front of several other women and children, Pierson raped Harriet. Private William Lindsey held Matilda to prevent her from helping Harriet. Afterward, Lindsey chased Matilda back to the house. She managed to knock him down to prevent being raped herself. Shortly thereafter, Pierson ran through the house with his pants down, warning Lindsey "yonder comes the head man of the plantation." Fearing the master, both men fled.

During the trial, both men objected to the women testifying against them on the grounds that "she was a black woman and was therefore incompetent to testify against a white man." The court disagreed. Both women were repeatedly subjected to resistance questions even after they had stated they had kicked and screamed. They were also extensively cross-examined by their assailants. Private Hugh Bragg, the third man, stated that he was not present the entire time. He testified to the good character of his comrades but admitted that Pierson "in some ways acted decent and in others he didn't." Both men were found guilty. Pierson received one year, hard labor and no pay for four months for the rape of Harriet McKinley, and Lindsey was sentenced to four months, hard labor and no pay for one month for his assault on Matilda McKinley.[20]

The court failed to call the victim during the court-martial of Private William Swift. Swift left his post and raped an "unknown woman of color." Captain James E. Roberson investigated the charges. He brought a doctor to the woman's house, where she was "crying violently." The doctor examined the woman and reported that she had been "ravished shortly before." Not only was the victim not called to testify, neither was the doctor. Swift was found guilty of other charges, but not rape.[21]

Privates Louis Trost and Lewis Sorg and a black servant, Jerry Spades, rode to the home of Mrs. Swindler, a widow who lived "in an out of the way place in the mountains" near Sperryville, Virginia. They asked her for some food. At first she was unafraid and gave them some "milk, bread, and honey." Pleasantries soon turned ugly. The men spotted two little Confederate flags, called Mrs. Swindler a "God damned secessionist bitch," and began plundering her home.

Afterward, the men went to the "darkeys house" looking for arms. Instead, they found Mrs. Swindler's slave, Polly Walker. Trost went over to her and said he "wanted to have something to do with me." He grabbed her and threw her on the floor. Polly said: "I cried, and struggled against it but he said if I didn't give up he would kill me. . . . I did not try to hurt him; didn't try to pinch or kick him; or pull his hair. . . He pulled up my clothes; I didn't try to keep them down, only begged him not to do it." Trost raped Polly and when he was finished, Jerry Spades followed suit. Only Sorg did not assault her.

In areas of occupation, military courts could try citizens alongside military personnel. All three men were charged with conduct prejudicial to good order and military discipline. The charge of rape for two of the three men came under a subheading, not as a separate charge in itself. Whether that was due to Polly's race or the fact that she admitted to halting her resistance when her life was threatened, the historical record remains silent. The men, of course, claimed that Polly was willing.

Trost was sentenced to hard labor for the rest of his enlistment, which amounted to two years, and given a dishonorable discharge. Being black himself, Spades received a harsher punishment of five years, hard labor. Sorg, the lone man who did not rape Polly, was given a one-year prison term.[22]

A fourteen-year-old girl, known only as Louise, walked along the sidewalk of Montgomery, Alabama, with some letters. Private James Deery of the 1st Louisiana Cavalry stopped her and asked her what she was doing. With the aid of Private Augustus Morrison, he dragged her into the blacksmith's shop. She tried to escape and cried. Deery asked her why she was crying, and she responded that she was scared. He said, "Dam[n] it I can make you get over your scare." He struck her with his fist and "pulled up my Clothes and got on top of me." He had unbuttoned his pants and "he tried to put what I saw into me."

Private John Richards was a guard patrolling the streets. Alerted to a disturbance at the shop, he found Deery in the process of what he thought to be "in the act of ravishing the Colored Girl." Morrison had kept watch at the door, and both men were taken to the guardhouse. Both men admitted to being drunk and not recalling what they had done while under the influence of whiskey. Deery appealed to the court:

> I have been four years a Soldier and never have violated any Military Orders until this time.... When at Home... I have always worked hard for a living. I submit my self to the generosity of the Court to do what they can for me as my Father has been killed in the War and all the support my Mother has is me.... I have been two Months in prison all but a few days and is a very hard place if I get out of this trouble I will not drink any more Whiskey.

Deery's plea was ignored. He was sentenced to five years, hard labor for conduct prejudicial to good order and military discipline, not intent of rape. Morrison received three years and was released three months later. There is no further record on Deery.[23]

In a case of obvious prejudice, Mary Hudspeth walked near a contraband camp with her niece, Lou. Private Isaac Cox of the 5th U.S. Artillery

Contrabands

called to her and told her to stop. Frightened by the encounter, Mary ran into some tall weeds but fell. Before she could get to her feet, Cox and another man approached her. Cox caught her hand and said that if she screamed "he would fill my mouth full of rocks."

Mary told Lou to run for help. Before anyone returned, Cox assaulted her.

> He pulled my clothes up; he took my breast pin off, he unbuttoned his pantaloons and climbed on to me. . . . This was about twenty yards from the Sutler's shop. . . . They did not give me any money. . . . There were eight men there but nobody did nothing but the prisoner [Cox] and one other man. The rest stood around and . . . looked on. When the prisoner was on top of me he pushed his "thing" into me; he shoved it as far as he could into me.

Mary specifically pointed out that no money was exchanged because if there had been, no matter how much force the men used, she would have been labeled a prostitute. After Cox assaulted her, the other man raped her while Cox held her down. He "put his hands over my mouth. He hurt my jaw and squeezed my throat so that I couldn't eat for a week."

At least two black men, Jim Ragslain and Samuel Hubbard, came to help Mary. Both men belonged to the 101st USCT Infantry and both saw two men holding Mary. Ragslain yelled at the men to "halt," and Hubbard raised a knife. Caught in the act, Cox and the unidentified attacker fled. Cox fell and offered Ragslain two dollars if he would let him go. He broke loose of Ragslain's grip, but fell again. Ragslain caught him again, but Cox screamed for help. White soldiers who had been watching the scene threw rocks at Ragslain and Hubbard. Undeterred, Ragslain turned Cox over to the lieutenant, where he was arrested.

Hubbard helped Mary, and "she throwed her arms around my neck. . . . She was so near choked that she couldn't say anything." Both men testified that she was a "decent woman" and hard-working. Mary's niece also testified, corroborating the testimony, but the Judge Advocate made this note afterward: "This girl 'Lou' is apparently about 9 or 10 years old—does not know her age and not very intelligent."

Two lieutenants, who had not been present during the altercation, testified that Cox was an "excellent soldier." The sutler owner stated that Cox had bought some notepaper from him, but could only approximate the timing. He thought it was "about the time of the hollering." In spite of two black male eye witnesses, Cox was found not guilty and set free. The other man escaped.[24]

John F. Herd, a former Missouri State Militia member, went to the home of Harriet Nelson. Along with three other men, Herd demanded that she hand over a government horse. Harriet denied that she had any such horse. Under the pretense the men were U.S. soldiers with orders to search all houses for arms, they went inside. Herd demanded money and he threatened the slaves. Two men began taking shawls, blankets, boots, a gold locket, sugar, glasses, and a jug of liquor. Afterward, Herd ran after a fourteen-year-old slave girl, Amelia Caroline. He caught her by the throat and raped her in front of her father.

Not only did Harriet, Amelia, and Amelia's father testify as to what happened that day, but a man who accompanied Herd also testified. He claimed that Herd and one other man had been involved in the robbery. Undaunted by the prosecution, Herd brought in several character witnesses claiming that he was at home on the day in question. However, the witnesses testimonies were inconsistent at best in an attempt to recall an event more than a year before. Herd was found guilty of robbery, rape, assault with intent to commit rape, and violation of the laws and customs of war. He was sentenced to fifteen years.

An all-too-common letter-writing campaign and petitions to the governor ensued concerning Herd's excellent character. One justice stated that he had known Harriet Nelson for around twenty years and "her character has never been that of a high minded and honorable woman, and since the beginning of this Rebellion she has been known only as a Rebel." In essence, he claimed Harriet had lied.

Another such letter writer tried to acquire a copy of the evidence in the trial. Unsuccessful in the attempt, he had "from good authority that there was not two of the witnesses that agreed in their evidence." He spoke the truth—at least in the case of the defense.

A Missouri representative stated that Herd admitted going to Harriet's house and tore up and scattered items. Herd's excuse had been that Harriet had abused him by calling him a "Lincolnite nigger thief." Not one letter or petition mentioned the raped girl, but they were forwarded from the governor to the president. Judge Advocate General Holt reviewed the case and noted the inconsistencies. He also stated:

> Both the robbery and rape are clearly proved, without the use of Mrs. Nelson's testimony—by one of Herd's companions in

the affair, and by the girl upon whom the rape was committed, besides several other witnesses.

The Commission imposed the minimum penalty . . . for the offense charged, which should . . . be enforced.

Holt's ruling was approved and the governor notified.[25] Because Herd was a citizen, there is no further record to verify whether he served his full term.

In Louisiana, Corporal William Chinock approached Mary Ellen De-Riley and claimed he had orders from the captain to take her to Fort Jackson. Complying with the request, Mary Ellen got aboard the boat that would take her across the river to the fort. Instead, the vessel headed upriver. Upon landing, the group went to a store, and the men started drinking whiskey. Mary Ellen complained that she should be taken to the captain, and on the return trip to the boat, Chinock knocked her in the head with his fist. He picked up a stick with the intent to beat her, but another man intervened.

Mary Ellen said, "He told me to lay down there and let him ride me and I told him that I would not." Chinock struck her again. Mary Ellen continued:

I was sitting down, and he came before me and shoved me over, and rode me. He had all my clothes up over my head. He did not know what he was doing. He entered me. . . . They were all as drunk as they could be. . . . He [Chinock] was so drunk he could not stand up. Could not stand without staggering.

One of the other men testified that he had heard her screams, and the captain, who did not witness the assault, stated that Chinock had always been a "good soldier."

Chinock was found guilty of "conduct to the prejudice of good order and military discipline." In other words, he was guilty of having "unlawful sexual intercourse," not rape. For his crime, he was reduced in rank to a private in front of the regiment and charged a fine—ten dollars a month for four months.[26]

On the night of March 21, 1865, several men went to the house of James B. Lewis in Kentucky. He wasn't home, but three women were. The soldiers said they were looking for one of the "boys." Lewis's wife, Sarah told the men that no other soldier was present. One man asked her "for some ass."

"Well, that is not my principle, sir," she replied.

"I have got to have it, and I be damned to hell if I don't have it." He pressed his pistol to her head. "I will be damned if I don't shoot you." Sarah escaped and went to a neighbor's house for help. Four soldiers escorted Sarah's eleven-year-old daughter Biddy outside where, she said:

> They took me . . . under a locust tree; they got up on top of me; they laid me down on the ground and pulled up my clothes, and said if I screamed they would shoot my damned brains out; the first man unbuttoned his clothes. After he had laid on me the other one got on me, too, and did something to me; he hurt me right smartly.

Lieutenant D.O. Bravard was the first man to rape Biddy and Private John Linville was the second. Biddy's mother had sought her husband, who returned with three men. When caught in the act, Linville tried to run. He halted when Biddy's father told the men to shoot. The two unidentified soldiers escaped.

Biddy went into the house with her mother. Her father soon followed. Inside, he examined his daughter. "She was bleeding and I told her mother that I thought she was ruined." Biddy bled for two days and could barely walk.

Neither Bravard nor Linville had any excuse for their actions besides being drunk. Both were dismissed from the service and sentenced to five years in prison. While military courts attempted to follow the laws of the state in which they were stationed during the war, making the eleven-year-old Biddy under the age of consent in Kentucky, the case remains unusual in the sense that an officer was sentenced as harshly as a private.

Closer examination of Bravard's military record, however, reveals that a petition was written on his and Linville's behalf from former commanding officers. The letter claimed there had been no evidence in the men's courts-martial, except for "the girl, and her recollection was *very uncertain*, and her identification of the accused was by no means positive." They also had been soldiers "of the fairest kind" before Biddy's rape and model prisoners in the interim. The former officers either were uninformed about what really happened during the courts-martial, or the rape of a young black girl was unimportant to them. Not only had Biddy identified Bravard and Linville, they had been caught in the act by others. Nevertheless, their opinion swayed the authorities. Both men were released from prison after serving nine months of their sentences.[27]

Henry Murphy had two cases against him for conduct to the prejudice of good order and military discipline. For striking a superior officer and drunkenness, he had the left side of his head shaved. His misconduct continued. While intoxicated, he joined several other soldiers in shooting off guns that injured a young "negro boy." He also pillaged a plantation. Sergeant James Ball was sent with two men to investigate. A black woman ran toward him. She was crying and relayed the details to him. When he went through the gate, "the lady of the house" called out to him, requesting protection. He proceeded to the slave shanties and found soldiers looting the houses. He convinced the men to leave, then he went to the next building. He found Murphy "on top of a negro wench."

Murphy told them to leave him alone, and for some reason they did. Ball claimed that he had his hands full with the drunken soldiers, but none of the men made any motion to help the woman, who they admitted was "scared to death." No one even bothered to learn the woman's name.

Ball stated, "She said he had been on her for an hour. She did not say anything about his taking hold of her and forcing her into the room. . . . She said that he had struck her in the face and kept hammering her in the face." He also witnessed Murphy's threats. Even though Murphy made "an up and down motion," Ball was uncertain whether there was penetration. After Ball and his men returned to the picket line, the captains sent them back to collect Murphy. The private was in the same shanty, alone and asleep. For the crime of violating a negro woman while intoxicated, Murphy was sentenced to be branded with an R on his left hip in the presence of the brigade. He was also given thirty days of hard labor, then drummed out of the service.[28]

In a drunken state, Lieutenant Charles Wenz of the 4th USCT Cavalry arrested an old woman's husband for no reason and ordered his sergeant to "blow his brains out if he moved." He then proceeded to the house where he walked inside, sat down, and asked for some water. The elderly Ann Booze obeyed his demand only for him to state what "other thing" he wanted. Ann jumped back and cried, "Oh no." She could not. She had a husband.

Wenz ordered Private Isam Jackson to catch her. At first the private refused, but Wenz drew his revolver on him. Ann fled the house, but Jackson caught up with her and carried her over to Wenz. The lieutenant returned Ann to the house and told the private to take care of the horses. He threw her on the bed, stripped her, and "ravished" her. Initially, Wenz was sentenced to a dishonorable discharge and five years. However, the sentence was not approved and he was granted a new trial. After the second trial, Wenz wrote in his defense that by law, "a Slave or freeman of color could not be guilty of rape on a colored woman, much less could a white man."[29] He continued with the argument, "Rape can be committed on the body of a white woman, *only*."

The Judge Advocate countered Wenz's argument that rape was governed by English common law, stating that rape is "the unlawful carnal knowledge of a woman against her will."

Wenz began his lengthy statement with the Matthew Hale phrase that it was difficult for a man to prove his innocence. He also claimed the prosecution had failed to make a case. None of the testimony had mentioned penetration or emission, nor whether his pants had been unbuttoned. In an attempt to show that no force had been used, he recounted Ann's testimony:

> *She would not do it,* not that she outdone him—not that she resisted his force, but mark the expression—*She would not do it*—then we conclude her *volition* was consulted, his amorous efforts were directed to win her consent, and not to force her... he teased her, and resorted to the extremity of means to excite her passions and win her consent.

He continued his defense:

> The *intention* of the accused was not to ravish, but to persuade and the testimony is so contradictory... as to leave it in doubt whether or not his passion was gratified... and he the accused is not guilty... for if he was gratified she was willing—and if not gratified then because he was unsuccessful in his amorous pursuits.

According to Wenz, the only crime he was guilty of was youth: "he was drunk—he was amorous, but he ruptured not the hymen of chastity—he committed no crime." He concluded his drawn-out argument by reminding the court how he had honorably served his country during the war and reiterated that a black woman could not be raped. Wenz was found not guilty of rape. For pointing a gun at an enlisted black man and assault and battery with intent to commit rape, he was given a dishonorable discharge and sentenced to two years, hard labor.[30]

Private Anthony Lander of the 113th USCT admitted to Private A.J. Jackson of the same regiment that he had "ravished" his wife. As well as assaulting, Elizabeth Jackson, Lander attempted to rape Susan Washington. He drew his knife, scraped her face, and cut her cloak. She screamed and drew the attention of three other men. Lander was found guilty of rape, assault with intent to kill, and assault with intent to commit a rape. He was sentenced to be shot, but the death sentence was commuted to ten years, hard labor. In the end, even that sentence was disapproved on the technicality that no plea from Lander had ever been written down. He was released from confinement and returned to duty.[31]

No serious testimony was heard in the case of Corporal A.C. Warner. He had been accused of attempting to rape Nicy Allen and clubbing John Allen (presumably a relative to Nicy). When John Allen was called to testify, the Judge Advocate objected to him being a witness on the grounds that he "had not the sufficient intelligence to comprehend the nature of an oath." Unlike many other courts-martial, the ruling held and A.C. Warner was found not guilty.[32]

In South Carolina, Privates Robert Corey and John Davis went to the house of Betsy Ladson. Corey asked her for a favor. She replied that "I could do no favors for him but to wash his clothes." He said she must "do it." Then they came into her house and Davis struck her with a walking stick on her wrist.

The following morning, the two men reappeared accompanied with two other soldiers. When Betsy spotted them, she went inside and locked the door. Corey knocked and asked her to let him in. When she refused, Davis took an ax and broke in the gable end. Davis held Betsy's feet while Corey threw her clothes over her head. He choked her to keep her from screaming. "After that he took his prick out and I felt it on my right leg."

Captain Kellam was alerted by "a colored boy coming to my Quarters, and telling me that some men from our Regiment were at his peoples house and committing Depredations." He went to investigate and discovered four men outside the house. "The woman of the house [was] crying, making much noise . . . and had the appearance of having been hurt." He summoned a sergeant and four soldiers and arrested the four men.

Corey was charged with absence without leave and conduct prejudicial to good order and military discipline, which included attempted rape. Corey called one of the other soldiers, James Jackson, as a witness; he denied everything, including Betsy crying. Inconsistent testimony by the defense and Captain Kellam's testimony were ignored. Corey was found guilty for being AWOL, not attempted rape, and sentenced to three weeks of hard labor. Davis was found guilty for being AWOL and contempt and disrespect toward his superior officer. He was sentenced to two months hard labor.[33]

These cases, involving Union soldiers as well as a couple of civilians, are not meant to be an extensive overview of the courts-martial involving the rape of black women, but a sample. The majority of the cases involved alcohol and the use of weapons. Of the courts-martial, three cases involved lieutenants and one an assistant surgeon, which was the equivalent rank. Among these four, one served no jail time, two were pardoned after serving a few months, and only one officer served a sentence longer than a year without a pardon. He was also found guilty for pointing a gun at another soldier. Overall, officers received very little sentencing for raping black women.

Four soldiers involved in this study were corporals. One was found not guilty, and two were reduced to the ranks and returned to duty. Only one, Corporal Hakes, was handed a sentence of two years. However, the charge on which he was convicted was not rape, and he was released after serving a year. Like the men from higher ranks, corporals were not sentenced harshly for the rape of black women.

The remaining twenty-one soldiers were privates. Private Isaac Cox was found not guilty. Four privates were found guilty for being AWOL or leaving their posts, but the rape charges were dismissed. One of these privates had his two-month sentence disapproved and was returned to duty. Another private received thirty days for violating a Negro woman. Privates Deery and Morrison were found guilty of other charges, but not rape. Morrison was released after three months of a five-year sentence, and there appears to be no further record on Deery. Private Linville received five years but was released after nine months. Private Clark also received five years, but the prison had no record that he had ever served any time. Clark's accomplice, Private Redmond, deserted and was never brought to trial. Private Tully died before serving his full two-year sentence. The single black soldier in this group initially received a death sentence, but it was reduced to ten years. Ultimately, he was let go on a technicality.

Seven privates appear to have served their full sentences. Private Pierson received a year, and Private Lindsey, who was guilty of attempted rape, received four months. Private Mitchell raped a ten-year-old girl and was sentenced to three years. German-born Private Trost received hard labor for the rest of his enlistment (approximately two years), and Private Sorg, who did not rape the victim, received one year. Private Killgore received the harshest punishment, ten years. He was found not guilty for rape, but guilty of assault with intent to commit rape. He also tortured his victim. Killgore's accomplice, who did not succeed in his rape attempt, received four years. In character with the era, most privates served reduced sentences to lesser crimes for the rape of black women. Even Killgore, who tortured his victim, served for assault with intent to commit rape, not rape itself.

The two remaining men in the courts-martial were citizens, and it remains unknown whether either served their full sentences. In the case of John Herd, there was a white witness, automatically increasing the seriousness of the crime, and he was found guilty of rape as well as other crimes. In all probability, Jerry Spades served his full sentence, as he was black and was the third man involved with Privates Trost and Sorg.

As in civilian courts, most men who raped black women were given light sentences. At the same time, the Civil War was a turning point: black women's voices were beginning to be heard.

Chapter Seven

"I Was Afraid They Would Kill Me"

White Victims

IN CIVILIAN RAPE CASES UPPER-CLASS WHITE WOMEN were more likely to be believed, especially if the alleged rapist happened to be black or a poor laborer. Poor women were less likely to reveal they had been raped because this often called their reputations into question, and they feared being victimized again by the legislative system. As in the previous chapter, examination of the Civil War military records shows a striking similarity to civilian cases. This will become evident as the cases are reviewed.

Reports also came from diaries. Joseph Waddell wrote in June 1864, "The wretches [Union soldiers] violated three females in Amherst [Virginia]—a young girl who died, and two married women." Clara Maclean told of her near-escape from being raped several years after the war. "Before I was aware of his intention, he had locked the door." With some quick thinking, she talked her way out of the situation by telling the soldier where the valuables were kept. "I measured him from cap to boots, then fixed my eyes steadily on his, not fearful in the least . . . only as I pressed my left hand against my side I felt there a strange, wild fluttering. . . . With the other I slowly and stealthily unloosed the stiletto from its sheath . . . and still gazed at him with unflinching nerves and tense muscles." Clara did not know whether it was her determination or that he had heard his companions galloping away that caused him to pause, but she said, "What do you mean, sir? Open that door!" For a minute, he hesitated, but then he unlocked the door and went outside.[1]

Newspapers tended to report more rapes of white women than black. In Maryland, a private "has been summarily ordered to be hung" for the rape of "Miss Carroll," a member of a well-known and influential family. No such execution in the court-martial records has been found. Bishop McGill of Richmond read the news in the paper. He had officiated the marriage of her brother, "grandson of the Carroll[s] of Carrollton," and knew her well. He wrote in a letter, "I hope there is some error in the account of the sad affair, and that she was not the victim of his crime."[2]

The *Richmond Daily Dispatch* reported that "Henry Rapur, a Yankee" had been received at Castle Thunder prison for the charge of rape. Castle Thunder was a Confederate prison in Richmond that housed mostly civilians, including spies and political prisoners. And a "Federal soldier" by the name of "McCoul" had "ravished a lady in Matthews county, Va, was sent to Hanover Junction... for trial by Military Court-Martial. He was seated in the cars with a chain and 24 pound ball on his leg, and his face showed the agony he felt at meeting his fate, about which there is little uncertainty. Death by hanging is the penalty of his heinous crime."[3] No record of either man is listed in the Union courts-martial, but if they were tried by Confederates, the records were likely destroyed during the burning of Richmond at the end of the war.

Emma Holmes read about a "sickening account" in the newspaper. One of the New York Zouaves (units that adopted North African–inspired uniforms) was arrested in Alexandria, Virginia. He allegedly went to the home "of a female of the highest respectability" under the pretense of "searching for concealed weapons." The woman had a six-day-old infant sleeping at her side and, the correspondent continued in a common Victorian fashion: "With any, save a demon, the prostrate and helpless condition of the lady would have protected her, but such considerations did not weigh with this... monster, and with the fury of a savage, he gratified his hellish lusts.... Screams of his victim attracted the attention of passers-by, and the villain was promptly arrested, carried before the commanding officer, and ordered to be shot."[4] There is no record of a New York Zouave having been executed in 1861.

Also in Virginia, Private Robert Christian was captured by the Confederates and was charged with "a most horrible rape upon the person of a female resident.... He was remanded for trial." The record has likely been lost with so many other Confederate records. In any case, Christian died a year later in the Confederate prison Castle Thunder.[5]

According to the *Daily Times* in Kansas:

Two soldiers of the 2nd Ohio Cavalry, and 10th Kansas, were taken recently from the Sheriff of Bourbon county and hung. Their crime was an outrage on the person of the daughter of Mr. John Davis one of the oldest and most respectable citizens of the county committed in the presence of the mother of the young lady. The popular verdict will be "served 'em right."[6]

Again, no record has been found of these two soldiers being executed, but the article suggests that by a sheriff being involved they may have been tried by local authorities or their deaths were the result of a lynch mob.

Some women fought back. According to the *Arkansas True Democrat*:

Six or eight of his men [Major General Samuel Curtis] went to the residence of a respectable lady (the widow of a true southern soldier, who died in the service,) and attempted to commit an outrage upon her person, and were only deterred from carrying into execution their diabolical intentions, by her drawing a repeater and firing upon them.[7]

Like black women, newspapers rarely named poor women. In the cases of upper-class women, male relatives were named as frequently as the victims themselves. As already pointed out in Chapter Three, the *Official Records* also reported cases of rape.

Private James Currance was caught "in the act of committing a rape upon an old woman sixty years of age" by two other soldiers. There is no record of a James Currance ever belonging to the First New York Mounted Rifles. However, names were commonly misspelled, and James H. Curham, belonging to the same company, deserted a few days after the recorded assault.[8]

From North Carolina, Brigadier-General Joseph R. Hawley wrote:

The authority of the Government is weakened and brought into contempt by the impunity with which stragglers, deserters from either army, marauders... commit outrages upon the inhabitants. To say nothing of insults and plundering, there have been three cases of rape and one of murder, to say nothing of rumors of others.[9]

Like newspapers, the *Official Records* rarely reported names. The lack of detail may have contributed to the trend of women's claims frequently being dismissed as hearsay. In reality, if the charge of rape actually made it to court, men who raped white women were usually given light sentences—just as for black women.

Thirty-two-year-old Anna Mason met two soldiers near Memphis, Tennessee. They had two canteens of whiskey and asked her to drink with them. When she refused, the two men dragged her around and beat her with their fists. Eventually, they tied her with a rope about her waist to a tree and raped her repeatedly throughout the night. Even after all of the abuse, Anna was asked if she had done all that she could "to prevent them from violating your person." Two days later, Anna died from her injuries in the city hospital. From her deathbed, she identified one of her attackers as Private Hugh Burns of the 108th Illinois Infantry and gave a final statement to Lieutenant Peter L. Eckley and several other witnesses. The second soldier was never found.

Burns was charged with murder, not rape and murder. After all, a dead woman could not prove that she had been raped. Anna's attending surgeon testified that her clothes were torn and saturated with blood when she was brought in. Her vagina had been lacerated and the neck of her bladder had been torn loose from the vulva. Not only had she been raped, but the men had also run some instrument "up into the womb." The doctor suspected a stick had been used because he had removed splinters. He also stated that Anna was rational when she had been brought in.

A private claimed he had seen Burns with a woman under a tree. She groaned but didn't ask for help. He failed to notice whether she was drunk or sick, and apparently did not think to ask her if she needed assistance. He also noted that Burns's hat was bloody. A camp washerwoman went on to say that Burns had brought her a bloody shirt and trousers.

The defense attempted to dismiss Anna's deathbed statement as being unreliable; either she had made a "false statement willfully and maliciously" or her mind was gone (a statement contrary to the doctor's testimony). He continued that Burns had always been of "habitual good character with the exception that he would *occasionally* get intoxicated and even while under the influence of liquor was of a mild and pleasant disposition—always peaceful never quarrelsome or malicious." In spite of the defense plea, Burns was given a dishonorable discharge and ten years. However, after Burns served time for a few months, twenty-six men from his regiment sent an appeal to President Johnson, claiming that Burns could not possibly have been the ringleader in the case, if at all. He also

had a wife and children at home who depended on him. Burns was pardoned, provided he returned to his regiment and served the remainder of
his enlistment. The Judge Advocate felt that Burns should have suffered
"no less than 'Hanging' " for such a "heinous" crime.[10]

In 1862 Missouri, three soldiers came to Susan Ward's house, where
she lived with her four children and Sarah Downing, her widowed mother.
Susan's married daughter, Rebecca Mitchell, lived nearby and was visiting at the time. The men claimed they would serve as guards for their
protection. One man insisted that Rebecca return home at once and that
he would accompany her.

Susan got her children ready in order to accompany her daughter
when the man said the guard would fire on the house if she came along.
Resigned to remaining behind, Susan had her twelve-year-old son, William
Ward accompany his sister.

Two guards remained behind. One man, Private William Evans of the
59th Illinois Infantry, said to Susan that he had come to "fuck" her. After
supper, he forced her against a door and raped her in front of her mother
and children. After the assault, Susan went over to the fireplace, sat down,
and wept. Evans ordered her to go to bed, where her children already
were. Before long, Evans's comrade dragged her out and raped her. While
Evans's comrade raped Susan, Evans had moved on to her eighty-year-old
mother. The elderly woman told the court what happened:

> He pulled out his penis and tried to put it into my mouth, threw
> me on the bed, and forced me to have connexion with him. I
> tried to push him off, resisted all that I could, but he was too
> strong for me. Said that he wanted to see "it" to see if "it" was
> as gray as my head.

After the comrade finished his assault on Susan, Evans returned. Before she could get to her feet, he "got on top of me and again had connexion with me. . . . I struggled and resisted him all I could."

Meanwhile, at the Mitchell household, Private Benjamin Davis of the
1st Missouri Cavalry sent Rebecca's brother back home. Sensing something amiss, brother William failed to do as he was told. He sneaked
around to the back of the house and listened through a crack. His sister
and her baby were crying, and he overheard Davis tell her to lie down;
she refused.

William called out to her, but Davis warned her not to answer. Eventually, Davis told William to go home or he would make him. Inside the

house, Davis told Rebecca that he was going to have "connexion" with her. Even though she had her baby in her arms, he pulled up her clothes and shoved her onto the bed. He made Rebecca lay the baby to her side before raping her. When finished with the assault, he forced her to turn toward him and raped her a second time.

After the second attack, Davis fell asleep and several other men entered the house. Rebecca covered her baby with some bedclothes. Fearing that she would be assaulted yet again, she said:

> [I] went down to the bank of the creek. The night was dark, and it was raining. I hid under the bank, where it was necessary to put my limbs into the water up to my knees, in order to keep out of view. I stayed in that position about two and one half hours.

During Rebecca's testimony, she was asked by the court if she had made "any effort to keep him from getting on top... such as holding your legs together or pushing him off." She was also questioned if she had "the same feelings that you have when in connexion with your husband?" Rebecca's husband, William, had been away from home until the night after her attack. The Judge Advocate questioned him about his wife's behavior as if she were his property and responsible for her rape, "What if anything did you say to her about *her* [emphasis mine] conduct?"

Privates William Evans and Benjamin Davis were found guilty of rape. The third man was either never found or the transcripts of his court-martial were misplaced or lost. The sentence for the two privates found guilty for a night of terror on three generations was to have their heads shaved and drummed out of the service to the tune of the *Rogue's March* in front of the Division. Their buttons were to be cut off, they would forfeit all pay, and if they were found within military lines again, they would be shot.[11]

In Alabama, Privates Joseph Halroyed and Frank Enger of the 1st Louisiana Cavalry got drunk and went to the home of Mary Bankister. Armed and threatening to shoot, the two men grabbed Mary and her sister Corine. When the women resisted, Halroyed said, "Shoot them God damn them. Shoot 'em Bring me a torch and I'll set the house afire."

While a defendant usually waited until his statement to counter testimony given during a court-martial, Halroyed openly denied the claim against him. In an unusual move, he said, "I didn't say a word about [a] torch. I said search the house and see if there's any rebels there and if there is, burn it down."

Regardless of what was said initially, the men forced the women into the house at gunpoint with a threat to shoot, if Mary "didn't submit to their wishes." Corine managed to escape and sought help. Before anyone came to Mary's aid, Enger raped her on the floor, then promptly fell asleep. Afterward, Halroyed raped Mary "four or five times." He made her take off her clothes and go to bed with him and said that "he was going to keep me in the house till morning." Soon, guards arrived at the door and ordered for it to be opened. Enger and Halroyed resisted arrest with a threat to shoot. Sergeant David Jackson warned that he would break the door down and, with the help of three other soldiers, succeeded in arresting the men.

During the courts-martial, Mary was asked how many inches each man had penetrated her and if they caused her any "pain during the operation." Halroyed denied Mary's testimony, then later admitted in his statement to the court that he remembered very little of the event. Both men were found guilty of rape and were sentenced to dishonorable discharges, the forfeit of their pay, and ten years, hard labor.

Halroyed made a plea soon after sentencing, stating that he was "a young man and made drunk by older and more experienced" men than himself. He felt he was led into the "horrible act," and because he was only eighteen, he would be "old and gray" if he suffered in prison for ten years. His record claims that he had been a model prisoner up to that point, but his request apparently fell on deaf ears. There is no mention in his military record of an early release.[12]

On the night of May 28, 1864, in Burnt Hickory, Georgia, Privates Charles Billingsly and William Cutsinger claimed to be guards of the provost guard and went to the home of James Smith. They informed him that he needed to accompany them to headquarters. The men had been gone for about an hour when Cutsinger returned to the Smith residence and told his wife Louisa that her presence was also required.

Once away from the house, Cutsinger led Louisa into the woods, pretending that it was the way to headquarters. At that same time, he called for "Charles." All at once, he seized her and threw her to the ground with the intent to "frig me right there or kill me." She fought him, but he grabbed her hands, pulled up her clothes, and raped her. After the assault, he led her to the road where they came upon "Charles." Again, Louise was thrown to the ground and this time raped by both men. They let her up and accompanied her back to the house, where both men raped her again.

At both men's trials, Louise was asked several times if she made all of the resistance in her power. To which she replied that she had, except in the house. That time, she said, "I just gave up, and made no resistance. I was afraid they would kill me." At Billingsly's trial, she was asked what she meant by saying that Charles had connection with her. "Did he insert his penis into your body each time?" After she responded in the affirmative, the court asked, "Could you have been mistaken about it?" The same questions were repeated during the Cutsinger court martial, along with: "Can you say positively that the accused inserted his penis in you in the thicket, on the road, and in the house?"

Billingsly and Cutsinger failed to remain quiet about their escapades and bragged to several other comrades at the 7th Indiana Light Artillery. Private Joseph McCoskey quoted Billingsly as saying, "Boys we had a good time last night, me and Cutsinger." He went on to say that the men had admitted to the deception. Two other soldiers corroborated McCoskey's testimony. Billingsly was called to testify during Cutsinger's trial and stated they had never been in the woods.

Both men were found guilty of rape and given a dishonorable discharge and ten years, hard labor. Both deserted to the enemy before the sentence was carried out.[13] However, Billingsly was recaptured. William Hartpence, a member of the 55st Indiana, wrote: "He refused to tell how often he had deserted, but substantially admitted a number of times. He confessed to the murder of a woman and her child, and was known to have used the names of Cooper and Miller as aliases."

Another report claimed that he had been known under several aliases. His sister visited him "the night before his death, but all she could get out of him was that 'if he died now, he'd be better off; he wouldn't have so much to answer for as he would if he lived longer.' " On December 23, 1864, Billingsly was shot to death by musketry. He was executed for desertion, not rape or murder.[14]

In Maryland, Private William H. Cole, 109th New York Volunteer Infantry, was charged with the rape of Olivia Brown, a fifty-year-old woman. After drinking heavily, he beat and raped Olivia. Her daughter witnessed Cole throwing her mother to the floor while "screaming murder." She ran to get help.

Lieutenant G.A. Matthews, who was looking for Cole, happened on the Brown residence shortly after the attack. He found Olivia crying; "the skin was knocked off one side of her face." Two other witnesses confirmed that she had a bleeding face. A fellow citizen was called to testify regarding her character. He stated that, after knowing her for six years, he had never heard anything bad about her.

In Cole's defense statement, he claimed Olivia's injuries were the result of a "battery, not rape. The injury done must be to the *private* parts in order to prove a rape." He also stated that "false accusations for rape are by no means rare." With no conflicting evidence, Cole was sentenced to ten years, hard labor.

Four members from the 109th submitted affidavits on Cole's behalf, claiming that Olivia ran a bawdy house. The colonel and lieutenant colonel also submitted a letter to Abraham Lincoln stating that "she supplied them with whiskey & where her conversation and conduct were well calculated to influence and excite to violence the passions of a drunken man." The captain of Cole's company also submitted a letter saying that Cole was a good soldier. His commanders made no denial of his guilt. Instead, they utilized the age-old tactic of demeaning the woman's reputation. Resorting to rape myths, they alleged Olivia was at fault for exciting Cole to violence. Regimental members used terms such as "lewd" and "bawdy house" in their letters in order to further place the blame on her. Thirty-five citizens signed a petition stating they had known Cole since childhood. He was a "good citizen, except that he was occasionally a little wild." Lincoln pardoned Cole and he was returned to duty.[15]

During the middle of February 1863, John Doyle, a private of the 15th Maine banged on the door of Lucretia Williams, waking her in the middle of the night. He demanded that she open the door or he would break it down. Armed with a gun and bayonet, he broke the door in and said he was "secret police," searching for "negroes."

With her husband, Captain James Williams, away from home, Lucretia allowed Doyle to search the house. Convinced that she hid no contraband slaves, Doyle gave "insults" and touched Lucretia. She "begged him to desist."

Doyle replied that "Yankees didn't do like Southern people—that they didn't seduce ladies and turn around and kill them." After raping Lucretia, however, he threatened to blow her brains out, if she had him arrested.

After Doyle left, Lucretia spent the rest of the night on the floor. When morning arrived, she fled to the home of a friend, Flora Ann Lard, and told her about her night visitor. Because she was too embarrassed or ashamed to tell Flora the details of the rape, her friend advised her to wait to report the incident to the provost marshal until her husband

Woman in camp

returned. Too afraid to remain alone, Lucretia asked a male neighbor to stay with her for a couple of nights after the attack. During that time, Doyle returned, once again threatening to break the door down. He also said that he would kill anyone who protected her. The neighbor was able to get away and reach a guard, who arrested Doyle.

During Doyle's court-martial, Lucretia was asked the usual resistance questions. However, many of them were more telling about the men on the court. "Did you lay quietly during the act of copulation, or did you struggle?" "Did he enter your person fully or partially?" "Did you resist by the use of your legs?" and "Did you resist to the extent of your strength with your legs, and how long did such resistance continue?" Such badgering questions went on for several pages of transcripts.

The court also asked Lucretia if Doyle had proceeded in "a violent manner." The rape was often referred to as "the affair." The court's questions hinted that the neighbor staying with her might have been an illicit affair, rather than a man helping a woman until the return of her husband. Undoubtedly because Captain Williams returned ten days after his wife's assault and no one had contacted him about it before then, the court suspected that no rape had occurred.

Doyle produced a witness who claimed he had watched the pair from the window. He admitted that Lucretia had given a scream "very low and very short," but she had gone to bed with Doyle with no hesitation. "I saw her clothes stripped up and her legs as far up as I could see decently, and saw the prisoner doing his duty."

In Doyle's statement to the court, he said, "Had I been tried while I was at Pensacola [Florida] I could have proved the character of this woman." He also stated that Lucretia had asked him for money, but he only had seventy-five cents at the time. "She said she would trust me until I came again." Once again, by placing the blame on a woman's reputation, Doyle was found not guilty.[16]

Not all black men who committed rape received harsh punishments. Accompanied by another soldier, Henry Duncan of the 4th USCT Heavy Artillery went to the home of Elizabeth McDougal near Pine Bluffs, Tennessee, under the pretense that he was searching for "guerrillas." Duncan inspected the lower story, but Elizabeth balked at his request for her to accompany him upstairs. The soldiers left without further incident. Frightened by the encounter, Elizabeth gathered her children together and went to her brother's house. Her thirteen-year-old son went to bed in the back room.

Between nine and ten that night, soldiers, including Henry Duncan, appeared at the Gardner house. They went to the room where Elizabeth's son slept. The boy told them to "go away." They threatened to "blow his brains out" and continued searching the house. The men came to the room where Elizabeth, her brother William, and his wife were. The soldiers shouted for William to give up his arms. Thinking that he was the target of their search, the women encouraged William to escape the house. He went out a window. Meanwhile, the soldiers pushed the door open. Armed with a gun in hand, Duncan grabbed Elizabeth. He pushed her on the bed, choked her, and raped her in front of her son. Her sister-in-law escaped the scene.

After the attack, she went to a neighbor's house, where her brother eventually found her. He reported the attack to the authorities, and Duncan was identified from the lines of soldiers as her attacker. Duncan was found guilty for being away from his post and sentenced to forfeit his pay for four months. There was no finding on the intent of rape charge.[17]

Also, in Tennessee, Mary Kirksey, a seamstress and washerwoman, had signed the "oath of allegiance" pledging her loyalty to the Union. She "had never mistreated a Union soldier and . . . no Union soldier had ever mistreated" her, until the morning of May 18, 1864. She was first visited by Private David Crutchfield in the belief that she was a "base woman." He spoke with her and came to the realization that she was "not that kind of woman." Before long, Private Charles Hunter of the 7th Kentucky Cavalry showed up.

Mary continued tending her wash outside, and Crutchfield left the premises after informing Hunter that he thought she was a "decent woman." Hunter departed soon after, but returned a few hours later. A neighbor dropped by and chatted with Hunter while Mary washed clothes. After the neighbor left to visit another sick neighbor, Hunter's friendly nature turned personal. He took hold of Mary. She scolded him and went to get her clothes because it had started to rain. Hunter helped her with the laundry.

Once inside, his touches became more intimate, then he pinned her left arm behind her back. He picked her up and carried her to the bed. Mary screamed and tried to kick him. He responded by slipping a leather strap over her mouth, gagging her completely. He threw Mary's clothes over her head and "nearly smothered" her, then raped her.

After the assault, Mary sat on the floor and cried. Hunter took her "pocketbook . . . and kind of laughed and said that he had a notion to rob" her. Later in the day, Private Crutchfield returned. Mary asked him "what kind of soldiers there were here." She relayed what had happened and showed him her bruises. He advised her not to report the incident because he thought Hunter would not return.

A captain who came later to collect his wash gave Mary the same advice. Other soldiers came for their wash and asked her what was wrong. She informed her neighbor of the assault. Contrary to everyone's estimation, Hunter reappeared a few days later. Mary's son happened to be there at the time, and Hunter pretended he needed directions.

Two days later, Hunter yet again appeared at her home. She was outside and tried to get away, but Hunter was faster. He grabbed her. Hearing her screams, a neighbor's young son came running and witnessed the scene. With a mix of threats and saying that he was going to marry her, Hunter asked for forgiveness. He said he was going to "cut her liver out" and called her a "Dixie Bitch," then said he wouldn't treat her so if she would marry him. Thinking quickly, Mary said she would think about it and give him her answer the following day. He was afraid it would be an "answer that he would not like." He shook her hand and kissed her, giving her money that she refused. After he rode away, she reported the incidents to the colonel.

In a rare set of court-martial transcripts, the court noted in several places that "the witness was here so affected that she could hardly give her testimony" and "the witness wept here bitterly." All of Mary's witnesses corroborated her testimony. Even Hunter's witnesses refused to soil her character. In an effort to damage Mary's reputation, Hunter wrote in his statement: "Crutchfield was trying to sleep with her and was angry because I interrupted him. I went away and came back again and I firmly believe that he had intercourse with her." He claimed his innocence and stated that Mary "has a reputation of being a base woman.... We were talking about getting married.... I have perhaps offended her and this is her revenge.... I have no witnesses and I am the victim of a scheming woman."

After being sentenced to eighteen years, Hunter appealed to the president. Judge Advocate General Holt held no sympathy for Hunter and felt that justice had been served. Even though Mary had waited a week to report the assault, her testimony was believed because she had several male witnesses who refused to let a woman's reputation be ruined. Hunter served a year and a half of his prison sentence before being released.[18]

Catharine Farmer was visiting her neighbors, the Howells, when Lieutenant Harvey John came along and said another neighbor had sent for her. She replied that she had a sore foot and would go when she was ready. John offered for Catharine to ride his horse, but she refused. The lieutenant left, and Catharine waited for about an hour before going to the neighbor's house. She walked a short distance only to find John lurking. Again, she sought refuge at the Howells. She waited about a quarter of an hour before leaving once more.

About halfway to her destination, Catharine spied John yet again and later told the court what happened:

> He told me to come out into the woods with him. I refused and he swore he'd make me. He laid hold of me.... I tried to jerk loose from him. He seized hold of me again.... Told me what he was going to do and that if I did not give it to him, he would kill me, right there. I told him I would die right there then. He pushed me backwards and got over me, he struck me once. I was hollowing, and screaming, he put his hand on my mouth

to try and stop me. He forced me. He held my hands with one
of his and pulled up my clothing with the other.

Lieutenant Joseph Siddell thought he heard a woman's cries. He rode
toward the sound and someone rode past him "pretty fast." Siddell came
upon Catharine, who was "crying and screaming." A few minutes passed
before she calmed down enough to tell him what had happened. He got
back on his horse and pursued John. Siddell caught up with him and
arrested him. Immediately, John claimed that Catharine had lied.

During John's court-martial, the defendant cross-examined Catharine,
continually asking her if she had agreed to meet with him. He also called
a couple of hand picked witnesses to testify that her character was bad.
Once again, Catharine had an important male witness on her side, and
John was found guilty and sentenced to ten years, hard labor. However,
John requested a continuance and in 1890 he wrote a letter to the Judge
Advocate asking for a copy of the findings in his case. His military record
states two different sentences—ten years for one and two in another with
a dishonorable discharge. Only history knows which term he actually
served.[19]

In a classic blame-the-victim case, Michael Shehan went to the home
of Maria Wade and asked, "if you have got any protection here show
me the damned son of a bitch." He drew his pistol and said to her that
"he would blow my damned brains out." Afterward he drew his bayonet,
then went into her house and searched the place. Her neighbor, Mary
Wiley, was present at the time, and when Shehan returned, he reached for
Mary, but she managed to escape his grip and run. Instead, he grabbed
Maria and threw her into the canal. The record is somewhat unclear,
with confusing testimony, but another man pulled her from the canal and
Shehan proceeded to rape Maria twice. Or the two men may have taken
turns.

Maria fully admitted that she was a poor woman with "no learning,"
and Shehan's counsel clearly took advantage of her lack of education by
continually asking her harassing questions. "And you tell the Commission
that this man without any provocation whatever and without any motive
in the words that you can assign took you up and tossed you in the canal?"
He also asked, "Don't you know that if you had exerted all your strength
you could have prevented that man having connection with you?"

When Maria testified that Shehan had threatened her life more than
once, not to mention that she had been recovering from being tossed in
the canal, the counsel asked, "And that is the estimate that you placed
on your virtue and you would not scream for a threat?" "You had your

tongue, a woman's great weapon?" "And that horrible outrage of a rape didn't overcome your fright so as to make you scream?" Again he asked: "Do I understand you to say that you submitted to him twice without saying a word?"

The arresting provost marshal claimed, "The matter about the rape was given to me in a confidential manner by Maria Wade, from the fact that... she felt ashamed." He also stated that she had claimed the man who had pulled her out of the canal had been the first to rape her, "and the prisoner afterwards." Initially, he had arrested two men in the case, but when the second man could not be identified, he was let go.

The defense counsel badgered all witnesses for the prosecution. However, Catherine Murphy, a witness for the defense, claimed that Shehan was "modest, decent, and honest." She also stated that Maria had invited Shehan to her home. The counsel asked if she was positive about this, to which she replied, "Do you think I would give a false oath?" Counsel accepted her response completely without any follow-up.

In Civil War military courts-martial, the accused never took the stand, but they did issue statements. In Shehan's case, his counsel submitted the statement, which started by using Matthew Hale's quote. He followed it with: "Can human credibility believe that she was ravished *twice* of a summer night, here in the City of Richmond, within less than a stone's throw of houses teeming with inhabitants?" He asked how unlikely it was for a young man to *want* to gratify his passion with a woman aged fifty years by making a joke with a poem about an "amorous youth... caught in his grandmother's bed." He also went on to state that it had been impossible for Shehan to have thrown her in the canal, as there was no motive because they were "strangers." If Shehan had truly meant to rape her, the counsel argued, he would have done so, *then* thrown her into the canal—not the other way around.

In describing Shehan, he said, "A demon would not be such a fool, and the very face of the accused shows that he is neither demon nor fool, nor murderer or ravisher either, but simply a gallant young soldier." The counsel's badgering of witnesses and illogical statements were enough to discredit Maria's testimony. Shehan was found guilty of assault and battery, but not rape. He was sentenced to nine months, hard labor.[20]

In an unusual case for the era, Mary Skidmore relayed that Corporal Jacob Bladner, Private John Williams, and another man had come to her house around ten o'clock at night. The men said they had delivered prisoners to Clarksburg, West Virginia, and then were unable to get through the picket lines. They claimed they would need to stay the night. Mary refused to keep them. She said the men told her that "if I would let them lie down before the fire they would behave themselves." She fixed up a bed for them and retired herself.

An hour later, "Jacob Bladner got up and come to my bed, and wanted to get in my bed." Mary held her child in her arms and begged him to go lie down. "He cursed me and swore he would fuck me . . ." She called her boy, who woke the other soldiers sleeping by the fire.

One man put on his boots and left, but Williams wanted a drink of water. There was little water in the house, so he went to fetch some. When he returned, he threw the water on the fire, putting out all of the light in the room. He then proceeded to pull the boy outside with him. Mary attempted to run, but Bladner caught her and threw her back. She struck her head against the wall. The blow momentarily stunned her, and Bladner repeated what he was going to do to her, then raped her.

The case is unusual because, beside Mary, the only witness called was the third man, who knew very little about the case. Her testimony stood on its own merit and she was never asked any resistance questions. Perhaps that was due to the blow to her head, but Jacob Bladner was sentenced to fifteen years for rape and John Williams was sentenced to eight years for his assistance in the crime. Williams escaped from confinement while waiting for sentencing and was recaptured, which likely gave more credence to the victim's testimony.[21]

In February 1864, after stealing approximately $107 from the Stephen Howard family, Privates William Jones and Horace Ralph of the 3rd Wisconsin went to the home of William Martin. Apparently with more theft in mind and dissatisfied that no money was to be had, Jones broke into the daughter's room while Ralph held Martin and his wife at gunpoint. Menesey Martin, Caroline's mother, struggled to aid her daughter, but Ralph pointed a gun at her and said he would "make a light hole through her." She continued to struggle and each time Ralph threatened her with death.

From the other room, Caroline's voice could be heard: "O Mother he is pissing on me." When Jones threatened he would have what he came for, Caroline said she "was no such girl." Stating that it made no difference to him, Jones grabbed her and threw her on the bed. He told her if she did not do it "he would kill my Father and my mother" and "burn us all up." The transcripts are unclear as to the specifics, but Caroline averted Jones's rape attempt by "resisting him." Jones was found guilty of robbery, assault with intent to commit rape, and plundering. Ralph was charged with holding Caroline's mother while Jones attempted to rape Caroline. Both men were sentenced to be executed. Ralph's sentence was commuted to five years, hard labor. Jones's was not. However, before Jones's execution was carried out, he escaped and was never recaptured.[22]

In April 1864, Sarah Jane Ledman was on her way home with two friends, Lizzie Fairfax and Martha Jane Fair. With a penknife in hand, Private Thomas Bond came down a bank onto the road and approached them. He told the women he had been to Richmond and spoke pleasantly to them at first. Soon his manner changed, and he said to Lizzie that he must arrest her and take her back to camp. The only thing that could save her is "if she would consent to that." Lizzie refused, and he "clinched" both her and Sarah. Lizzie escaped and shouted for help, while Martha stood in place and screamed. Meanwhile, Bond threw Sarah to the ground and threatened to cut her throat if she screamed. "He threw me down and done just as he pleased with me."

Two men came down the road and Bond ran. The two men testified to finding Bond's knife and that he hadn't been in Richmond. Bond was sentenced to fifteen years and given a dishonorable discharge.[23]

In May 1863, Mercy Whippey traveled from New Jersey to Virginia in order to care for her wounded son. Lieutenant George O'Malley was assigned to protect her. At first he seemed gentlemanly, but that changed one night when she was alone in her tent. O'Malley entered around eleven at night and woke Mercy by saying "good evening." Mercy had been sharing the tent with another couple as well as O'Malley, and initially she was not alarmed.

He proceeded to pull off his boots, take off his coat, and lie down on a separate cot. Then he asked Mercy if she was comfortable. She complained about the woolen blanket. O'Malley insisted that she use his blanket. Afterward, his questions started to become personal: he asked her why she did not wear a night dress. He was more than willing to help her change.

The lieutenant got into bed with Mercy and pinned her to the bed. When she asked him what his wife would think, he replied that "what his wife did not know wouldn't hurt her." Mercy struggled against his grip and managed to break loose. She ran for help. Several witnesses testified that Mercy was barefoot and very frightened after the incident. O'Malley claimed that "he was innocent as any child in the whole matter." He had taken a couple of drinks beforehand and had fallen while trying to make her comfortable. He also stated "that he was the son of a General in the British service, in which he himself had served there for twenty three years, and now that he had enlisted in the defence of this country rather than go back dishonorably disgraced he hoped the Court would shoot him."

O'Malley's plea was ignored. He was dishonorably discharged and sentenced to six years, hard labor. However, President Lincoln pardoned him after he had served four months.[24]

In Louisiana, sixteen-year-old Georgiana Josephine Bryan was driving cattle out of her father's field because both of her parents were sick. Private Evan Williams of the 48th USCT approached her and asked where her father was. He then said that he wanted to "do it" with her. He followed her and knocked her down, telling her that he would kill her if she made any noise, and raped her.

In his defense, Williams admitted that he had asked her what he wanted, and she had simply laid down. He claimed: "She did not try to prevent me from having sexual intercourse with her. She screamed a little but I told her to hush, when she stopped and did not make any more noise, or try to resist me in any way." Williams was found guilty and sentenced to be shot with musketry. He escaped before the execution could be carried out.[25]

The case of Private Perry Holland is rare because most men did not admit to raping a woman. Holland plead guilty to the rape of Julia Ann Anderson on April 24, 1863. As a result, there was no testimony; Holland asked for "mercy." He was sentenced to be shot, but even a man who had admitted to the crime did not receive the harshest sentence. The president commuted his execution to hard labor until the end of the war. Holland deserted four months later.[26]

In July 1862, Peggy Pumpkinpile and Betsy Dennis went to a nearby camp to sell onions. Along their way, Private Henry Scott of the 9th Kansas Cavalry sat on a log. When he saw the women approach, he laid his pistol beside him. They got closer and he inquired about the onions. Peggy insisted the produce was already spoken for. Scott offered "four bits for them," then caught Peggy by the throat and said he would give her "four bits to go into the bushes with him." He also told her that her "old man" wouldn't find out. Peggy refused. He picked her up and threw her down in the bushes. Betsy screamed and ran to get help.

Peggy resisted and managed to keep Scott from raping her. He picked up a silk handkerchief that Betsy had dropped and choked Peggy with it. Once again, he threw her down and put his foot on her "bowels." He unbuttoned his breeches and punched her in the belly with his pistol—but when he heard picket guards, he ran. In Scott's statement, he claimed that he had given Peggy half a dollar for sex and that she wanted to "do it" in the woods. Scott was found guilty of violating the rules and articles of war. He was sentenced to be shot, but the sentence was disapproved. He was let go on the technicality that the charges were too broad.[27]

Lieutenant Francois Wallenus became intoxicated and told another soldier's wife exactly what he wanted to do to her, if the other soldiers would hold her. Wallenus and Sergeant Charles Lutz grabbed her by the arms and were leading her toward their quarters when a boy on a horse went by. The woman, referred to as Mrs. Brown, called out to the boy, and Wallenus ran.

A number of soldiers testified to Wallenus's state of drunkenness, although some downplayed as to how drunk he was. The sergeant claimed Mrs. Brown became insulted for no reason at all, and Wallenus was found not guilty of attempt of rape. Judge Advocate General Holt was disturbed by the sentence. He wrote to President Lincoln:

> The proof is positive. The testimony of the lady herself being uncontradicted and unimpeached—that the prisoner [Wallenus] most grossly insulted her, taking hold of her, and telling the enlisted men if they would hold her, he would "force her." Beside this outrage, the conduct of the accused in drinking with and furnishing whiskey to enlisted men, and his intercourse with them is sufficient in itself to demand his summary dismissal.

The president gave Wallenus a dishonorable discharge.[28]

In May 1865, Private Thomas Ennis rode to the home of Mary Harris in Warren County, North Carolina, where her two daughters also resided. Mary asked for him to take pity on "us poor folks." He went into the house, took down the gun from the door, and poured out the powder, then asked for revolvers. Mary told him there were none. He asked if any of the women would "answer his pleasure with him." If they did not, they "would fare bad."

Mary replied that he would not want anything from her. "She was an old woman with a heap of children." Ennis then said that "if that young woman there would, it would do." Mary's daughter, Caroline Neal, stated that she was no young woman and married. None of that mattered to

Ennis. He put his hand on Caroline's shoulder and guided her to another room. He locked the door behind them, and only then did he put his gun down. He "helped" her onto the bed and raped her.

On the same day that Ennis raped Caroline, he robbed Henry Egerton of some boots and a gun. He also attempted to rob Richard Madden of his horse. Madden had a gun and escorted Ennis to the guard, where he was arrested.

During Ennis's court-martial, Caroline was repeatedly badgered by Ennis in cross-examination. He suggested that her mother had said she should "consent—as that would save them from any trouble." He also asked her if she put her arms around him when they were on the bed together, which Caroline denied. Mary corroborated Caroline's testimony and told the court that "she looked as white as a piece of cotton. She looked . . . powerfully scared." She admitted that Ennis had used no force, but threats of death.

Interestingly, in this case, no force was used in the robberies, only threats—as in Caroline's rape accusation. Ennis's statement to the court contained pages of documentation defining rape, including Matthew Hale's quote. At no point did he deny what had happened. Instead he claimed that

> the prisoner threw his arm (gently it may be) around Mrs. Neal, and conducted her, without violence and without opposition to another room, and helped her upon the bed. In regard to Mrs. Neal, it is proper to remark that her conduct throughout. . . was not that of a pure and virtuous woman, whose chastity had been violated. . . . It is clear according to the . . . law that when the woman submitted to the man, for the purpose of saving her home from robbery, that it would not be a case of rape. . . . Mrs. Neal only yielded from fear of death.

Ennis, whose real name was John W. Dodge, was found not guilty of rape. According to the law, Caroline had submitted out of fear for her life, but she had not been raped. Ennis was found guilty for both charges of robbery, even though Henry Egerton made no resistance due to threats on his life. He was sentenced to two years, hard labor for robbery, but never served the time. According to his records, he returned to duty on July 18 and mustered out of his company on July 21, 1865.[29]

After two weeks of scouting in Kentucky, Lieutenant Charles Helton got drunk and went to the Spence home, where he thought he would be able to spend the night. Once there, he proceeded to partake in a couple of more drinks, "cut up," and fired a pistol. The Spences refused to let him stay the night, and he escorted Zelphia Spence toward camp at gunpoint where he attempted to persuade her to be "as a wife." Zelphia escaped, and Helton went to the home of Captain Thomas Russell. The captain was away at the time, and Helton told Russell's wife, Jane, that her daughter was a "pretty fine girl." He then asked the daughter if she would go with him. When she replied in the negative, he said if she did not go with him he would "shoot her damned brains out."

The daughter ran off and hid, and Helton turned his attention to Jane. He caught hold of her, tore her dress open, felt her breasts, and said, "I have been on Scout fourteen days, and by God I must have you for my purpose now." Jane attempted to retreat to the safety of another room. Helton kicked on the door and shouted, "If you do not open the door, I will blow your God damned brains out."

Jane managed to get away from Helton and saw three men approach the house. She called for help. Two of the men said they wanted nothing to do with Helton because he was a "mean man." The older man in the group stayed out of fear that Helton might "abuse" or "kill" Jane. Soon after, Helton left the Russell house.

Helton was charged with assault and battery with intent to commit rape, conduct unbecoming an officer and a gentleman, and drunkenness while on duty, to which he plead guilty on all charges. The case is unusual due to the fact there was testimony after Helton plead guilty. His counsel's statement to the court used drunkenness as an excuse, plus the belief that Helton thought he was in a house of "ill fame" at the Spence house.

Counsel continued to say that

> gentlemen who enter disreputable places do not always con-
> duct themselves as gentleman should. But such forgetfulness
> is always itself forgotten when the gentleman emerges from
> these questionable places and resumes his place in his proper
> sphere. . . . The accused accidentally became so intoxicated, he
> in fact became so drunk that he afterwards had no recollection
> of what transpired. In that condition he may have committed
> some indiscretions, but he certainly had not criminal intent.
> The accused had a wife and children at home anxiously await-
> ing his return.

In other words, boys will be boys. Lieutenant Charles Helton was found guilty on all charges, except for drunkenness while on duty. He was not on duty during his state of intoxication and was sentenced to be reduced in rank as well as three years, hard labor. The reduction in rank was disapproved because of an irregularity: the court had proceeded with testimony after Helton had plead guilty. In this particular case, Helton made the mistake of singling out another captain's wife, and the women involved had male witnesses. He served less than two years of his sentence.[30]

The case of Private Anton Herter is difficult to comprehend. He was accused of attempting to rape six-year-old Anna Haegle and "unlawfully abusing a female child." Dr. McConaughy examined Anna shortly afterward and testified:

> [I] found parts swollen and tender. No injury done... I don't believe prisoner attempted to commit a rape. Same effect... could be produced by feeling of the vaginal parts with the fingers. No internal injury.... Same effect might possibly be produced by an attempt to introduce the penis, but if an attempt had been made to enter with the penis the parts would doubtless have been injured to a greater extent.

Two other witnesses testified that Herter had been drunk and had grabbed Anna. One stated that Herter had "played" with the girl. Both agreed that she had started crying and run off. Herter was found not guilty of both charges and acquitted. Apparently drunkenness was a legitimate excuse for sexually abusing a six-year-old girl.[31]

As in the cases pertaining to Union soldiers raping black women, these examples are not meant to be an extensive overview. Again, drunkenness and the use of weapons were fairly common in the attacks. Of the courts-martial, four cases involved lieutenants. One was found not guilty, and two were let go after serving a few months. One officer, Lieutenant John, served either two or ten years; the records are unclear. In this particular case, the victim had a male witness. In these small samples, there is very little variation between the sentencing of lieutenants for the rape of black or white women.

One case involved a corporal. Jacob Bladner, served his fifteen-year sentence; he had injured the victim. His accomplice, Private John Williams, was sentenced to eight years, and had escaped the guardhouse while awaiting sentencing, lending more credence to the victim's testimony.

The remaining twenty cases involved privates. Two privates were found not guilty outright. Six privates were found not guilty of rape or attempted rape charges, but were guilty of other crimes. Three of these privates were pardoned after serving a few months. The sole black soldier in this group was sentenced to forfeiting his pay for four months.

Five privates were initially sentenced to be executed. One private's sentence was disapproved, and he was let go on a technicality. Another private had his sentence commuted to hard labor, but he escaped from jail before the sentence was fulfilled. Two others escaped before they could be executed. The final private in this group had his sentence reduced to five years. Of these five, only two privates were found guilty for the sole crime of rape. One had plead guilty; the other was a black soldier.

Nine privates remain in the courts-martial overview. Two privates were drummed out of the service. Another two privates received sentences of ten years or more but were pardoned after serving a little more than a year. Two other men were sentenced to ten years, but they deserted to the enemy. One was recaptured and executed for desertion.

Only three privates served extended sentences. Two men received ten years, hard labor after they resisted arrest. In this case, the victim had male witnesses. The remaining private was sentenced to fifteen years. Two men had caught him in the act of rape, lending their testimonies to corroborate the victim's.

Overall, more soldiers were given lengthier sentences for raping white women than for raping black women. At the same time, few men served their full sentences. The victims of the soldiers who failed to receive early pardons had male witnesses. As in civilian cases, courts-martial centered around how much force men used and women's resistance and consent. Upper-class white women were believed more often; poor women often had their reputations brought into question.

Chapter Eight

"I Was Near About Dead"

Gang Rape

GANG RAPE IS A COMMON WAR PRACTICE. The strict definition of gang rape is a crime in which one person is sexually assaulted by several assailants in succession. Some studies include pairs, as well as three or more attackers. For the purpose of my overview of rape during the Civil War, pair rapists were included in previous chapters, although some cases could have conceivably been included under the heading of gang rape due to the nature of the assaults. Brief accounts of gang rape have already been mentioned in Chapter Three, and those soldiers who were executed for the crime were discussed in their respective chapters.

Men in gangs tend to lose their self-awareness and individual responsibility, especially when the members are in uniform. Gang rape is often committed by the members of the group in order of rank. In that way, rape becomes a bonding practice between the men, creating loyalty and camaraderie. Some men who would not ordinarily rape during peacetime participate in gang rape out of fear of being punished or expelled from the group or because there is little fear of consequences, since rape during wartime is rarely prosecuted.[1]

On April 28, 1864, Grace Barnes, a free black woman, was carrying a load of laundry on her way home near Pungo Bridge, Virginia. Three men, including Private James Halon, approached her, and were soon joined by two others. They asked her if she would give them a "diddle." When she replied that she would not, Halon asked her to go into the woods with him.

She refused, and one man took her by the arm and whirled her around. Private Nicholas Kane held a stick and threatened to kill her if she did not go into the woods. Soon after, they forced her into the woods and "throwed me down. Some of them held me down, and the others done what they wanted." Five men, Privates James Halon, Nicholas Kane, Edward Pickett, William Cahill, and John Brennan, all from the 20th New York Cavalry, took turns raping Grace. Two men, Halon and Kane, raped her three times each, and Brennan and Pickett raped her twice.

The other men laughed and threatened to kill her when she screamed. "The savage looking man [Kane] took hold of my legs, and held me, and stuck pins and sticks into me, because I would not lay as he wanted me," while the other men raped her. As the five men took turns, Sergeant Owen Curren sat off to the side of the group. At one point he said, "For God sake let the woman get her breath." After the gang had finished with Grace, she pleaded with Curren to let her "go home, that I was near about dead." He cursed her, threw her down, and raped her.

The following day, Grace returned the laundry and again saw several of the men. Halon called her "Sally," asked her how she felt, and when was she going to give him another "diddle." She replied, "Never."

Even though she was unable to control her urination for months after the attack, she was questioned by the court if she still suffered violence. During the courts-martial, the men took turns testifying for each other in their defense. All admitted to sharing the same jail cell and "agreed to tell how it happened." Their story was that Grace had been "perfectly willing" and there had been no violence. The men also claimed that Grace had prostituted herself, yet she never asked for any money. They felt no shame in their actions because, according to them, Grace had gone with them willingly.

In spite of almost carbon-copy testimonies, Halon testified that he was unsure whether Cahill had "connexion" with Grace. "She asked him if he would do it to her standing up against the tree" with which Cahill did not agree. Halon's testimony then shifted, and he said he believed that Cahill was the last man "that had connexion with her." In addition to rape, Halon was charged with assaulting a guard and striking and threatening to shoot a superior officer. He was found guilty of all charges and was sentenced to be shot by musketry. The rape charge was disapproved. A report came from headquarters:

The only proof there is in charge of rape that the connection with this woman was without her consent, comes from the woman herself. There is not the slightest corroboration...so far as violence is concerned. There is no evidence from any other person that she made any outcry at the time and no evidence from any other person that she made any complaint at any time afterwards.

For some reason, none of the witnesses to whom Grace had reported the crime were called during the hearings. Halon's sentence was mitigated to three years, hard labor and a dishonorable discharge for his other crimes. Due to uncertainty as to whether Private William Cahill had taken part in the gang rape, he was returned to duty. The other men were sentenced to dishonorable discharges and given various hard labor terms from three to five years. All sentences were commuted and the men returned to duty.[2] The courts had allowed the men to gang up on Grace a second time and make her relive the rapes through the justice system.

About an hour before dawn in May 1865, five or six drunken soldiers broke down the door at a home in Montgomery, Alabama. Penny Robinson, a black woman, lived with several other people, but unfortunately for her, she was nearest to the door at the time. One soldier caught her dress, another her waist, and another her hand. They flung her on the floor and four of the men took turns raping her.

From the other room, Frances Robinson heard Penny scream, "Don't kill me, don't kill me," before she fled in fear of her own life. Another house resident, William ran for help and got the attention of Lieutenant John Richards, the captain of the guard. He told the lieutenant that some soldiers were "ravishing" the women.

Accompanied by a corporal and two men, Richards investigated the disturbance. He stationed a guard outside each door, then went inside the house through the back room. Two soldiers appeared to have run off before his arrival, but he found four soldiers attempting to make a hasty exit. Penny had her "dress partly torn off in front." She "seemed to be in distress" and told Richards that "she had been abused and forced by those men."

Privates G. Hoopengarner, Mark Tulley, Josh Childers, and Lewis Sappington of the 52nd Indiana Infantry were arrested. Three of the four admitted they had been intoxicated and remembered nothing of the event. Sappington gave no testimony in his defense. All four were sentenced to five years, hard labor. Hoopengarner escaped prison a couple of months later, but in this case, a black woman was believed because she had a white male authority to testify on her behalf.[3]

In Kentucky, eight black citizens decided to look for "rebels" and surrounded the home of James Carroll. Dow Nailin "demanded weapons and greenbacks." They broke into the home and "had a right smart scuffle" with his daughter Susan. While guarding Carroll with a gun, other men joined in and held Susan down.

"They took hold of me. Mashed my mouth till the blood ran out of my nose and choked me. . . . There were four of them who forced me." The scene took place in front of her family. Nailin and George Narin were found guilty in a military court for guerrilla activities and rape. Both were sentenced to hang, and five thousand people attended the public execution. Three other men were tried for the charge of rape, but no one testified to the charge and they were found not guilty.[4]

Besides calling the victim a "Negro girl," not much was written about her in the case of Benjamin Wilson, a citizen teamster for the 6th Missouri. The girl's master testified on her behalf. He stated that four men came to his house, including Wilson. They stole some items, then headed to the slave cabins. The men proceeded to haul one of the girls out and rape her. The court asked if she resisted.

Wilson was found guilty of several crimes, including rape. He was sentenced to thirty days, hard labor. Headquarters felt the sentence was "too light," but it was approved. Private Lamber Webster was also identified as one of the men at the residence, but he was not charged with rape. The other men were not identified.[5]

Most gang rapes never made it to trial, but occurrences were mentioned in diaries, newspapers, and the *Official Records*.

Reverend George Whipple reported from Fortress Monroe in 1862 that

> four [Union] soldiers . . . went to the house, in which resided two colored men . . . and their families. A colored woman from the neighborhood was in the yard. . . . Two soldiers stopped in the front yard, the other two came to the house. Those outside seized the woman in the yard, each in turn, brutally violated her person, while the other two stood guard with sword and pistol ready for use.
>
> Of the other two, one stood guard at the door, while the other, after a terrible struggle ravished the young woman in the house, in the presence of her father and grandfather. . . .

The grandfather and girl came to the Tyler House, and told us the sad story of their wrongs... But there was at the time some fifteen thousand soldiers at Newport News, among whom the four have not been identified.[6]

General William T. Sherman's occupation of Georgia and the Carolinas, mentioned in Chapter Three, is a period of note. More gang rapes during this time were reported in people's diaries.

During the destruction of South Carolina, Emma Holmes wrote that "the negroes were so ashamed they could not bear to tell. The wretches [Northern soldiers] staid there a week & gave themselves loose rein in the most indecent manner without the men daring to interfere to save their wives."[7] A person only known as McCarter also wrote from South Carolina:

> Soon after the pillage began the frightened negro women sought earnestly protection and places of refuge, against lustful soldiery and even abandoned their little property to get under the protection of some efficient guard. The bodies of several females were found... stripped naked and with only such marks of violence upon them as would indicate the most detestable of crimes. In an army of 30 or 40 thousand men there must

The ruins of Columbia, South Carolina

have been some mere brutes, who took to the vocation when the town seemed abandoned to the unrestrained license of half drunken soldiery—to gratify their base passions on the unprotected females of both colours. I would cast a veil over this part of history of the fall of Columbia.[8]

Also from Columbia, a physician, Dr. Daniel Heyward Trezevant, reported instances of rape. Mr. Shane's "old negro woman" was gang-raped by seven soldiers. One soldier proposed they "finish the old Bitch." The woman's head was held underwater, and she was drowned. Trezevant also claimed that a Miss Kinsler had been "brutally ravished" by three officers and went crazy from the assault. Other accounts in Columbia mention fathers fighting off soldiers in order to save their daughters. One man with the help of a Union officer rescued "two young women" from a couple of "ruffians."[9]

The *Richmond Daily Dispatch* reported a similar account from Tennessee: "They [Union soldiers] are turning women and children out of their houses without food or shelter. They had ravished four young girls of good respectability in society, two of whom had become deranged." A Pennsylvania newspaper, the *Republican Compiler* recounted yet another from Westmoreland County, Virginia. Some black troops went to the home of a Private George of the 9th Cavalry Virginia. "Six negroes violated the person of Mrs. G. eleven times . . . being also sick at the time, with an infant at her breast." According to another report, "She is now almost a maniac, and begs that someone will kill her." In the same march, female slaves assisted white women to keep from being raped, and a Mrs. Belfield fought off her attackers with a whip and escaped to the woods.[10]

Another report of a woman going mad after being raped came from Céline Frémaux Garcia in Louisiana. She stated that a girl by the name of Carrie was taken from her home by "Yankees" while her grandmother was tied to her bed. The next morning, someone heard the woman groaning. Several citizens joined in a search when they heard what had happened. Carrie "was found nearly dead, and completely crazy . . . bathed in her own blood, disheveled and torn." Several months later, Carrie's father, who was a Confederate soldier, was able to visit. "What he found was worse than death: the beautiful babbling idiot for ever and ceaselessly begging for mercy; or laughing a frightful laugh at the bloody spots that she fancied were yet on her garment."

Such a response in a time when a "respectable" woman would have been regarded as damaged goods would likely have not been uncommon.

Céline also knew of another girl who had been raped, but she never learned the details. Only that "Ada... seemed to have grown older all at once, and I never saw her laugh after that time."[11]

In October 1863, Arabella Speairs Pettit wrote in a letter to her husband:

> Virginia Shields... gives the most awful account... She has been in Memphis ever since it was taken.... She *saw* from her window a Lady of the highest respectability taken in the broad daylight and stripped naked in the street and then her person *violated* by 10 drunken Yankees.[12]

Several instances of black women raped by Union soldiers in front of their mistresses were reported. The *Savannah Republican* wrote about an incident in 1862 Alabama: "The soldiers have been guilty of the most brutal treatment to the negro women in the presence of the their mistresses, and if their masters interfered they were shot down." In 1863 Louisiana, Brigadier General William Dwight Jr. mentioned in his report that much pillaging was going on. He considered the "scenes... disgraceful to civilized war." Houses were destroyed, and there were rampant stealing and threats to women's husbands. "Negro women were ravished in the presence of white women and children. These disgusting scenes were due to want of discipline in the army, and to the utter incompetency of regimental commanders."[13]

In the summer of 1864, General George Stoneman was unsuccessful in his attempt to free Union prisoners from the Confederate prison Andersonville. His men plundered along the route in Georgia in their attempt to reunite with General Sherman in a foray that became known as the Stoneman Raid. They stole goods and burned property. The *Charleston Mercury* reported what happened in the private sector:

> The officers exercised no restraint over them [soldiers] and even some of them joined those under them in committing acts of lawlessness. They entered private houses... broke open drawers and trunks.... In many instances house girls were ravished in rooms before their mistresses, and in yards in front of the houses.[14]

In 1865 on the Oliver plantation in Louisiana, Union soldiers entered the house. They remained in the dining room all day, where they consumed all of the food and wine. They also "called in the female servants... whom they compelled to share in their debaucheries, to assist in

the pillage, and to minister to their pleasures. The more refined maid servants fled for protection to their mistresses, to whose private apartments
they were pursued by intoxicated ruffians, who, with drawn sabres, and
using indecent and opprobrious epithets, drove them forth."[15]

Two Arkansas newspapers reported that seven men from the 14th
Kansas Cavalry and one from the 6th were charged with "torturing four
respectable ladies over a slow fire till they were horribly mutilated about
their heads, shoulders and feet and with ravishing them." Mrs. Seth How-
ell was identified as one of the victims, and one man was also charged
with "additional crimes upon the body of one of the victims which pen
would shudder to record."[16] One can only guess what crimes could have
been worse than mutilation and rape.

The Arkansas *National Democrat* stated at a later date:

> A band of fifteen or twenty men... visited several houses
> where the women and children were left alone. Gold was de-
> manded.... The women replied they had no gold.... After be-
> ing shamefully outraged, these fiends caught the women and
> held their feet on burning coals.... In some instances, they
> obtained small amounts, but carried their tortures to such an
> extent that one woman died, another had her leg amputated,
> and several others were burned to the knee so badly that they
> will be cripples for life.... Worst of all, an officer... and the
> Rev. Mr. Hutcheson, an ex-chaplain are implicated.[17]

Unless the records have been lost, only Private Robert Atwell has a
court-martial file, and he was tried for a robbery that involved a major. He
was found not guilty. The remaining men, including Atwell, have records
of being arrested at the time of the newspaper articles, but their military
records give no specific details. Sergeants John Mills, Adam Scott, and
Wisner Condra were all reduced in rank to private. Private William B.
Farmer deserted shortly after the incident, but most of the men appear
to have mustered out with their regiment in June 1865.[18]

In a similar story from Tennessee, three men from the 2nd Tennessee
Mounted Infantry, a Union regiment, went to several homes and robbed
them. At William Johnson's house, they demanded money from his wife,
since he was not at home. When she told them she had no money, "they
hung her and her daughter several times, completing their diabolical work
by each of them outraging the person of Mrs. Johnson." Lieutenant James
Bromley was placed in charge of the investigation due to the fact that he

personally knew the soldiers and the witnesses "by whom the facts can be proven." No record of any courts-martial or reprimand appears to exist. One of the accused, Private Thomas Brewer, had deserted for several months prior to the incident with only a loss of pay. It seems that these three men were allowed to rob several citizens and gang-rape a woman without any consequences.[19]

The *Official Records* contained reports of rape. General D.C. Buell had little tolerance for acts of violence against citizens. In fact, he was the commanding officer to bring charges against Colonel J. B. Turchin, mentioned in Chapter Three. In August 1862 in Alabama, he demanded the arrest of the officer who was in charge of a party who had destroyed property, arguing that "negro women are debauched, and ladies insulted." In Missouri, soldiers stole goods, searched houses, and were "committing rapes on the negroes." In Virginia, similar experiences took place involving black troops. "Twelve or fifteen [women] escaped almost miraculously from successful violence, and four at least became unfortunate victims of their brutal lust."[20]

Newspapers reported gang rapes. From western Virginia (present-day West Virginia), "a most diabolical outrage" had been committed on one of the "most respected ladies of Mercer county by five of Lincoln's fiends." The *Memphis Daily Appeal* also used the word "fiends" when describing the atrocities perpetrated. Besides stealing horses, arson, and murder, "rape is to be added. Five respectable females were the victims of these brutes."[21]

In Arkansas, a plantation had been plundered with one widow tied on the floor; her slaves were threatened if they gave her any assistance. "Another lady was seized by six of the soldiers, who successively accomplished the last outrage upon the sex, and left her helpless." Another assault in Arkansas was reported in true Victorian fashion in describing the victim. She was "educated, talented, witty and accomplished in a high degree. . . . Five abolition soldiers, including an officer, forcibly seized this young lady, carried her to a barn, and each of them committed an outrage on her person. In two or three weeks she died, a victim to their brutality."[22]

In Virginia, stealing and plundering were again mentioned. Soldiers captured an overseer, then stole watches and clothing from the slaves. They were also "guilty of a brutality so gross, so revolting, so horrible, that the pen of the chaste writer must be withheld. Suffice it is to say that an aged servant woman had to stand, with a drawn sword at her breast, and witness with an anguished heart the repeated defilement of her child, a girl about seventeen." Also in Virginia, a raiding party "committed rapes on three respectable ladies."[23]

In April 1864, Confederate General Nathan Bedford Forrest led an attack on Fort Pillow in Tennessee. He demanded surrender; Major William Bradford refused. Nearly half of the 550 Union soldiers were black, and only sixty-two survived. Debates still rage as to whether the taking of the fort was a massacre. In any case, people living in the Union of the time viewed it as such. At least one report stated that black soldiers avenged Fort Pillow:

> In one instance, the grandmother, daughter and grand-daughter were each in the same room held by the drunken brutes, and subjected to outrages, by the bare recital of which humanity is appalled. A young wife, *enciente*, taken to a negro encampment, and tied to stakes, driven in the ground, was made to minister to the hell-born passions of a dozen fiends. Death, in his mercy, came to her relief.[24]

Many newspaper articles were written for shock value, to anger soldiers into taking up arms against the enemy. Some stories made reference to countless women being ravished, but in reality most reported specific numbers, lending the articles a certain amount of credibility. Perhaps a Union deserter said it best to a Confederate general as to why he had deserted: "General, I have seen a party of these [Union] soldiers rape a mother and her daughter, with my own eyes." Upon hearing the story, Colonel R. A. Cameron of the 34th Indiana Infantry said to the general, "I was fully satisfied it was a base fabrication, for if such an occurrence had taken place it would have been known among us, and I had never known of it, and that a man who would desert would tell a falsehood." When the general went on to tell Cameron about the plundering that had taken place, he admitted that such things had happened, but he was satisfied that such conduct "was not with the consent of commanding officers."[25]

Like some historians, the colonel had turned a blind eye to the realities of war. Gang rape during wartime is not uncommon, nor was it during the Civil War.

Chapter Nine

"He Did It Against My Will"

Confederate Rapists

DUE TO THE LOSS OF MANY RECORDS during the burning of Richmond in 1865, fewer accounts exist of Confederate rapists. Some men were tried by the Union military as citizens, but all were also tried for being guerrillas.

In Lousiana, Omer Boudreaux was charged with murder, robbery, violation of the laws and customs of war, and rape. On May 15, 1865, the war had officially ended, but some guerrilla groups remained at large. Boudreaux and five other men entered the home of Joseph Verret looking for ammunition. They searched the house and discovered a powder horn. After rubbing Verret's face in the powder, they threatened to kill him. They also stole clothing, money, a blanket, a hat, a coat, razors, and buttons. Then they escorted Verret outside. All of the men left the house, except for Boudreaux. Five children remained inside another room with Artemis Verret. Artemis wanted to accompany her husband, but Boudreauz restrained her by the arm. He took her over to the bed. She wanted to call out, but he said if she did not let him "do what he wanted," he would kill the both of them. On the bed, he raised her dress and raped her.

During the testimony, one man who had ridden with Boudreaux stated, "She is a colored woman that is all I know—what I could hear she had a very bad reputation." When pressed on how he knew anything about Artemis's alleged reputation, if he had met her only the night before, he replied, "Several persons... I cannot name any one." The defense also attempted to place doubt on Artemis's reputation by asking her if she took "part in the intercourse."

"He did it against my will," she answered. "I did not enjoy it." In addition, she was asked if she had responded to "his exertion—with similar movements of your body?" Again, Artemis denied any wrongdoing.

Boudreaux was found guilty of murder, rape, being a guerrilla, and violations of the laws and customs of war. He was sentenced to hang. On October 27, 1865, President Andrew Johnson commuted the death sentence to life in prison. However, Major General Edward Canby released Boudreaux.[1]

In Tennesse, Union Major-General Milroy reported:

> A guerrilla... murdered two of my scouts, shot a number of loyal men, robbed them of everything they had... ravished one loyal lady, with fifteen of his gang, and made a similar attempt on an orphan girl sixteen years of age in the same room with the corpse of her cousin, whom they had killed.[2]

Abe Hendricks was arrested. Testimony from a number of citizens verified the general's report, yet none of them named Hendricks as having been involved. Most had known Hendricks since he had been a boy and stated they would have recognized him.

The Judge Advocate conversed with Mary Hall, the sixteen-year-old girl's aunt. She stated the girl had known one man involved, but he had not been Hendricks. Martha Marshall submitted an affidavit. She claimed that "she did not know any of the parties who committed acts of violence upon her person... if the accused had been one of the party she would have recognized him at the time." Hendricks went free.[3] The citizens might have been too afraid to name Hendricks, but unless more records are uncovered, it will always remain a mystery.

Another Confederate guerrilla in Tennessee was Thomas Hooks. Accused of many crimes, including murder, robbery, and rape, he was found guilty of most of the charges, but not rape. Three men went to the Fitzgerald home. Two white men masqueraded as black men and searched the house, stealing some blankets, thread, and coffee. They placed a noose around Amanda Fitzgerald's husband and threatened to hang him. The men also asked about the servant "girl," Susan Brannon. Each man took Susan into a another room separately and raped her. During the trial, Hooks objected to Susan being a witness on the grounds of her race and "deficit of understanding." The Judge Advocate ruled that race was no grounds in a military court and the "witness is neither an idiot nor a lunatic." Susan was allowed to testify.

At thirteen years old, Susan had some difficulty grasping the questions being asked of her on the subject of sexuality. She did not understand what was meant by "carnal knowledge," the basis behind any rape charge of the nineteenth century. She stated in simpler terms that she had been "frigged." Pages of testimony covered whether any of the men got "it in" and how far. Regardless, Susan was bruised and bled for a week because of the assaults. Amanda Fitzgerald verified that Susan had been badly bruised and was bleeding after the attacks. Either due to Susan's misunderstanding or because no deep penetration was actually involved, Hooks was found guilty of assault with intent to commit rape, but not rape.[4]

An editor at the *Louisville Journal* created a fictitious "girl guerrilla" by the name of Sue Mundy. The twenty-year-old Jerome Clarke who wore his hair long and had smooth-faced features assumed the role of Sue, and his band became known as Mundy's Gang. A couple of Confederate guerrillas charged with rape rode with the infamous Sue Mundy. One member was Samuel O. Berry, commonly referred to as One-Armed Berry who lost his arm in an accident before the war. He had become a schoolteacher and lived with the Shakers. At home, he watched in horror as a Union soldier bayoneted his sister when she tried to keep their grandfather's heirloom revolutionary sword from falling into the soldiers' hands. She lingered for five days, and Berry swore that he would revenge her death.

When Berry was caught by the Union, he was charged with robbery, murder, and two counts of rape. Two black women were the victims. One was only known by Laura. She was upstairs in a house when Berry and three men entered the premises. She described him as a one-armed man, who came upstairs holding a gun. He ordered her to lie down and raped her. During her testimony, she was grilled: "How could he ravish you if he kept a pistol in his hand all the time?" He also gave her a quarter as he was leaving, which she kept. The fact that she kept the quarter automatically made her testimony worthless: they regarded her as a "lewd" woman. The other woman, listed as Susan Lee, never testified. Berry was found guilty of his other numerous crimes and sentenced to death. After being inundated with letters and petitions, President Johnson later commuted his sentence to ten years, hard labor. At the age of thirty-six, he died in prison.[5]

Henry Magruder also rode with Sue Mundy and One-Armed Berry.

Born in 1847, he turned fifteen before he learned that he was an illegitimate child. He lived with his uncle and aunt and joined the Confederate army at the age of nineteen. He fought at Fort Donelson and Shiloh before joining with Mundy.

After the war, besides the charges of being a guerrilla, he was accused of murder and rape. Catherine Raymer informed her family, including her father, that she had been choked and raped. However, during Magruder's hearing, she swore no rape had occurred, nor could she identify who had choked her. The Judge Advocate abandoned the rape charge

> because after examining the principal witness I was convinced, either the woman had told a falsehood, and had not been outraged, or, that even if she had been, her testimony was false, and an outrage upon such a woman was not so great a crime as to make any difference in this case.[6]

No one will ever know what really happened, but Catherine had gone as far as to tell her family that she had been raped, giving her the prerequisite for believability that an attack had taken place. According to modern sources, the recanting of such testimony is not uncommon for numerous reasons, including fear of revenge and distrust of the legal system. Recantation *"does not* equate to a false report." Investigations should be held as to the cause of the change of testimony, rather than further the victim's humiliation.[7] Many of the Confederate guerrillas were in their home territory and knew the residents. In this particular case, a woman likely became too frightened to identify her attacker or ashamed to declare that she had been raped. In any case, the Judge Advocate dismissed an alleged rape as "not so great a crime."

Interestingly, according to Watson and Brantley, the biographers of Sue Mundy, an anonymous letter to Major General John Palmer stated that the widow of William Fox could identify Magruder and that Catherine Raymer and her sister were raped when Magruder's men stopped at Philip Raymer's house. The letter went on to say that six ladies were also raped by guerrillas while they were at school. No other evidence was found.

Magruder was hanged for several counts of murder. A newspaper described his execution:

> After his arms and legs were tied, and he was placed upon the fatal trap. He was asked if he had anything to say, to which he replied in the negative. The rope was then placed around his neck, and the white cap drawn over his face.... The trap

was sprung. . . . He struggled for some five minutes, and after twelve minutes he was cut down. . . . The crowd made a rush for the scaffold to procure a piece . . . or a strand of rope . . . used in the execution.[8]

John Brothers and another man known only as "Texas" also rode with Samuel Berry and Henry Magruder. In April 1865, Mary Clark traveled to a neighboring town on a mission for medicine when the guerrillas caught up with her and returned her to her home in order to rape her. The two men started a rumor that another guerrilla band that included Frank James (brother to outlaw Jesse James) was responsible for the crime.

Major General John Palmer immediately issued "Special Order 64." The order put everyone in the area on notice that no guerrillas would be allowed to surrender until the "perpetrators" were arrested. Frank James was furious that his group had been accused of the crime and about Palmer's subsequent order.

With a group of men, James tracked Brothers to a house where he and three men were dining. James threw open the door and said, " 'Keep your seats, all of you; keep your hands up; keep your eyes to the front.' Brothers . . . snatched swiftly for his pistol. Frank James blew his brains out across the table." Texas was not among the men at the table, and the guerrillas went in search of him. They claimed to have found him and killed him, which is incorrect. Samuel Berry and another guerrilla surrendered Texas to General Palmer. After the attack, Mary had described Brothers to the authorities, but there was not enough evidence to hold Texas on the rape charge.[9]

The band of John Nichols and James Johnson was among the smaller groups of guerrillas in Missouri. In late 1862, they had one other man riding with them when they went to the home of Frances Keam. They were cordial to her, but wanted the "Negro girl" at the home go with them. Frances said no because she was the only "help" she had. They insisted she would accompany them and would not be harmed.

Once away from Frances, they asked the slave girl if Frances's husband had any money. When the girl replied that he did not, Nichols said, "God damn you we will punish you then." All three men got off their horses and raped her.

Neither Nichols nor Johnson were charged with rape, but with being guerillas. Frances Keam testified for the eighteen-year-old girl, who was never named and referred to as the "girl" or "negro girl." Johnson was found guilty, but his death sentence was repealed. Nichols was executed on October 30, 1863. The third man was never named.[10]

One of the few surviving records from Confederate courts-martial is that of Private John Duncan of the 3rd Tennessee. From a summary of the record, he was found guilty for absence without leave, illegal and outrageous assaults on a citizen, and brutal assaults on a woman with attempted rape. He was sentenced to twenty-five years, hard labor. However, he was released and returned to duty.[11]

More Confederate rapists can be found in newspapers. Near Nashville, Tennessee, a party of guerrillas from Dick McCann's command went to the home of an unnamed citizen.

> [They] violated the persons of his wife and daughter in the most brutal manner. The ruffians, whose lust and revenge were still unsatiated, leaving this scene of horror, went to the house of a highly estimable widow in the vicinity and treated her in the same fiendish manner.

A follow-up article stated that the assaults were "a more aggravated case" than had been reported because "one of the sufferers is a girl not fifteen years of age." The article also claimed that another woman had been raped by guerrillas just a few weeks before.[12]

During the Gettysburg campaign of 1863, a newspaper reported that a Miss Worst had been raped by "rebel soldiers." In Maryland, the following year, the 8th Virginia Cavalry was said to have left "several . . . ravished women on their route."[13]

Several cases appeared in the local courts. In Richmond, Frederick McSweeney and Patrick Sullivan were "charged with making a lascivious attack on an aged negro woman, named Eliza," and James Phillips was acquitted from a similar attack on "Martha Jane Miller, a white girl, under 21 years of age." Three soldiers belonging to the McCulloch Rangers from New Orleans broke into the house of Clara Coleman and Lizzie Hubbard and allegedly "committed an outrage upon the person of a 'phrail phair one,' named Eliza Liggon."[14]

Near Portsmouth, Virginia, a member of the Polish Brigade was found guilty of rape by court-martial and was awaiting execution. Along with three others, he went to the home of a farmer "whom they securely tied, and afterwards took forcible and improper liberties with his wife."[15]

Also in Virginia, Confederate Colonel W.H. Wallace, 18th South Carolina Volunteers, reported that "instead of gathering up stragglers the soldiers were running about plundering and gathering up property abandoned by the enemy, and that almost every crime has been perpetrated by the command from burglary to rape." He went on to state that unless the matters were investigated, the War Department would insist upon an examination because "a most respectable lady" had been raped.[16] His statement implied that if any woman besides a "respectable lady" had been raped, the War Department would have been uninterested in the report.

A similar incident happened in Kentucky. Clergyman Jack Montgomery of the Kansas Cavalry was visited by the Border Ruffians. In a raid, "they took him prisoner, tied him to a tree, and brought out his wife—an educated, accomplished lady—and violated her person in the presence of her husband." Also near Jackson, Tennessee, a group of guerrillas belonging to "Faulkner's band" visited "an old man named Gordon." They made prisoners of him and his daughter. "They carried them to the nearest woods, and tying the father to a tree ten of the villains successfully violated the daughter. Gordon was then hung by the neck to a tree, and would have perished had not a party of Federals opportunely passed that way."[17]

A woman from Georgia received a letter from her husband that he had deserted the Confederate army and lived in Indiana. He wanted his wife to join him. "She started on foot, with several children." Along the way she met another woman "on the same errand." After walking a few miles, "they were met by a gang of rebel fiends. . . . Both women were subjected to the most horrible outrages. Not satisfied with this, one of the gang, who was infuriated by the resistance made by one of the women, shot her, killing her almost instantly."[18]

Private William Esry had a history of assaulting women. He attempted to commit a rape on a married woman near camp. George Griscom wrote about the incident in his diary: "A guard was sent for him, he was brought to Camp & whilst the officers were consulting what to do with him the boys *en masse* took him from the guards & hung him, buried him & distributed his outfit among the most needy of the company." Another report stated that Esry had shot another woman the previous year "because she would not consent to marry him."[19]

Confederate Brigadier General Wirt Adams wrote to a major about a group of soldiers who had stolen some supplies. He sent a party to arrest the group, but two of the men were sent to headquarters with two women and "detained these ladies all night in a camp . . . offered them every indignity, and are supposed to have violated one or both of them. The ladies themselves complained that every indignity was offered them."[20]

Few newspapers seemed to think that Confederate rapes against black women were noteworthy. One example was another guerrilla by the name of Bill Anderson. The infamous outlaws Frank and Jesse James rode with Anderson during the war, but in October 1864, Anderson, along with a company of his men, went to the home of Ben Lewis. Upon their arrival, Anderson and his captain demanded money from Lewis, then pistol whipped him. Both men shoved the barrels of their guns in Lewis's mouth. They proceeded to shoot at Lewis's legs and began a night of torture. During this time, they "took a negro girl, 12 or 13 years old, into another room and both of them ravished her by turns—one torturing Lewis while the other was committing the outrage on the negro girl."

The following morning, the group returned. Neither Lewis nor his wife were at home. Disappointed, they demanded breakfast for forty from Mrs. Clark. The slaves had been scared away the previous night, and Mrs. Clark was alone, except for a nurse who cared for Mrs. Lewis's baby. Anderson made Mrs. Clark send for a couple of servants "who cooked their breakfast, and after this was done, Anderson's men outraged the two women . . . and told them if Mrs. Lewis had been there they would have treated her in the same way."[21]

A Union prisoner of war, Louis F. Kakuske, relayed his experience in his memoirs. On his journey to a makeshift prison, his three captors kept their carbines nearby. At one house, the farmers served them a meal, and afterward they rested on the lawn. A middle-aged black woman came outside and the three Confederates eyed her. Kakuske described her as "a bit buxom" but "not unattractive."

The Confederates called her over. Since she was a slave, she obeyed. Kakuske watched in horror as each man took his turn raping the woman. Afterward, one turned to him and said, "Now, Yank, it's your turn." Kakuske refused to take part, and the Confederate threatened him to take his turn or be shot. Again, Kakuske said no. The men released the woman, saying that slaves were only good for two things: "work and to serve as concubines."[22]

Because so few records of Confederate rapists exist, few conclusions can be drawn. However, similarities to Union records do exist. A woman had to prove she had been raped. Her resistance and consent against a man's force were important for an accusation to go forward, and black women were considered to be little more than chattel.

Conclusion

"He Said He Would Blow Me to Pieces"

IN MAY 1863, PRIVATE EDEN HILL OF THE 10th MISSOURI and Private J.J. Sparks of the 4th Iowa Cavalry were sent on a mission to find a deserter. Near Keokuk, Iowa, they stopped at the home of Isa Parish, the father-in-law of the deserter, and arrested him. Hill told Parish's ten-year-old stepdaughter Sarah to come out of the house and show him where her brother was. Parish objected, but Hill pointed his pistol at Sarah. The girl headed toward a field while Sparks guarded Parish.

About halfway across the field, Hill sat under a tree and asked Sarah to join him. He then said, "lye [sic] down." Sarah refused and recounted what happened next:

> He drew his pistol half out and told me if I did not lie down he would shoot me; so then I layed down. . . . He put my head by the side of the tree, and spread my legs out. He then unbuttoned his pants and took something out and then layed down on top of me an[d] hurt me.

The Judge Advocate asked, "How did he hurt you?"

"He hurt me by putting something into me. So then I screamed and he jumped up." Suddenly frightened, Hill returned to the task at hand of searching for Sarah's brother. Sarah continued her testimony: "As we went along he told me if I didn't wipe the blood off my legs he would shoot me, and so I wiped the blood off my legs and heels as much as I could with leaves."

Contrary to what Hill had instructed Sarah, she reported the assault to her brother, and he accompanied her to the Parish house for clean clothes. At that point, Private Sparks let Parish go, and together they searched for Hill. As soon as he was captured, he was turned over to the provost marshal. Several hours later, a doctor examined Sarah and confirmed that she had been raped. At first he feared that she might die from blood loss. Confined to bed for three days, Sarah often woke crying from the pain.

During the Civil War era, even a ten-year-old girl could have been viewed as partly responsible for tempting men. The usual resistance questions were missing from Hill's court-martial, but Sarah was asked if Hill had offered her anything to "lie down" or if she had taken "hold or touch with your hand the thing the prisoner put into you." Hill was found guilty of rape, burglary, theft, and desertion on two occasions. He was sentenced to be shot. In spite of overwhelming evidence against Hill from witnesses within his own regiment, Sarah's brother and stepfather, and a doctor, the rape and burglary charges were dropped on a technicality: the locality where the offense had taken place was not listed. Although the desertion charges remained, while waiting for execution, Hill deserted yet again and "was last heard from was in the employ of the Hudson Bay Company."[1]

The subject of rape during the Civil War is a confusing, complex topic. Those who maintain that it was a low-rape war have not studied the subject during the era. Rape was rarely prosecuted during the nineteenth century. Even young girls, like Sarah, had to prove that they had not consented to the act, and women found it necessary to guard their virtue with their lives.

Young, unmarried women who had been raped were considered to be damaged goods and unmarriagable. While upper-class white women were more likely to be believed, many men maintained the belief that respectable women would have been too ashamed to admit being raped. The women who bravely came forward were often victimized yet again in the legal system.

In civilian courts, white men were rarely prosecuted, especially those from the upper class. The same holds true during the war. In war, women have commonly been tortured, murdered, and raped, but more often wartime rapes are carried out by small units and individuals. The cases that make their way to courts-martial are usually during times of occupation, where women can seek out an authority to report the crime and officials have the time to acquire the number of officers necessary to hear the crime. Women's chastity reputations are frequently put at stake, while men's reputations as soldiers are generally considered more important than any accusation of rape.

Contrary to popular belief, rape is not a crime of passion, but one of fear, power, and violence carried out in a sexual manner. The *Official Records* are riddled with claims of rape in the same breath as arson and plundering, yet only the crime of rape, a crime that was considered to be committed solely against women in the nineteenth century, has been dismissed as being rare. In fact, women's accounts have been dismissed as hearsay and propaganda.

In modern day wars, rape is rarely reported due to shame and a lack of faith in the justice system. The same held true during the Civil War, but women, like the slave mentioned in the Introduction, came forward in an attempt to seek justice. Susan testified:

> He took out his revolver and said, "God damn you, I will force you to do it." He said, "Don't say a word, you'll have to do it." He put back his revolver and then drew it again. I told him I couldn't do it. I was so situated [nine months pregnant] I couldn't do it. He cocked his revolver at me and cursed me. He said he would blow me to pieces if I didn't let him do it. . . . He came then and put his hand on my breast and pushed me over on the bed. . . . He told me to hurry and do what I was going to do. I told him I wasn't going to do anything. He said, "If you don't do what's right, I'll bust you open." I told him to let me alone that he hurt me. He said he didn't care a damn if he did. He got on top of me. He entered my person with his private member as well as he could. He completed the act. I was lying on a trundle bed. He used force.[2]

When a man aims a gun and threatens a woman with rape, she should *never* have to prove the assailant used force or answer endless questions on how she had resisted his advances in order to guard her virtue. Such interrogations were common during Civil War courts-martial.

No proof exists as to whether rape was rampant, as rape survivors generally remained silent. The *Official Records*, newspaper articles, diary entries, and court-martial records only skim the surface of the number of rapes committed. To assert that Victorian mores somehow imposed gentlemanly "restraint" during wartime is preposterous. Women—black, white, and Indian—were raped in greater numbers than most people care to admit.

Notes

Introduction

1. National Archives Record Group 153, file MM 2407 (hereafter cited as National Archives RG); and Compiled Military Service Record (hereafter cited as CMSR) Private Adolph Bork.

2. Bell I. Wiley, *The Life of Billy Yank, the Common Soldier of the Union* (Indianapolis: Bobbs-Merrill, 1952), 205.

3. Joseph T. Glatthaar, *The March to the Sea and Beyond: Sherman's Troops in the Savannah and Carolinas Campaigns* (New York: New York University Press, 1985), 72-74.

4. George C. Rable, *Civil Wars: Women and the Crisis of Southern Nationalism* (Urbana: University of Illinois Press, 1989), 160-161.

5. Michael Fellman, *Inside War: The Guerrilla Conflict in Missouri during the American Civil War* (New York: Oxford University Press, 1989), 201 and 209.

6. National Archives RG 153, file MM 2900.

7. Fellman, 207-214; and Michael Fellman, "Inside Wars: The Cultural Crisis of Warfare and the Values of Ordinary People," *Australasian Journal of American Studies* 10, no. 2 (December 1991): 1-9.

8. National Archives RG 153, file MM 1021.

9. Reid Mitchell, *The Vacant Chair: The Northern Soldier Leaves Home* (New York: Oxford University Press, 1993), 104.

10. Susan Brownmiller, *Against Our Will: Men, Women, and Rape* (New York: Simon and Schuster, 1975), 88-89.

11. Mitchell, 104-106.

12. United States Army Surgeon General's Office, *The Medical and Surgical History of the War of the Rebellion*, part 3, vol. 1, 3rd Medical Volume (Washington DC, 1870-1888), 891-896.

13. Mitchell, 106-110; and Joseph T. Glatthaar, *Forged in Battle: The Civil War Alliance of Black Soldiers and White Officers* (New York: Free Press, 1990), 118.

14. Stephen V. Ash, *When the Yankees Came: Conflict and Chaos in the Occupied South, 1861-1865* (Chapel Hill: University of North Carolina Press, 1995), 200-201.

15. Catherine Clinton, *Tara Revisited: Women, War, & the Plantation Legend* (New York: Abbeville Press, 1995), 129.

16. Ervin L. Jordan Jr., "Mirrors beyond Memories: Afro-Virginians and the Civil War," in *New Perspectives on the Civil War: Myths and Realities of the National Conflict* (Madison, WI: Madison House Publishers, 1998), 158; and Martha Hodes, *White Women, Black Men: Illicit Sex in the Nineteenth-Century South* (New Haven: Yale University Press, 1997), 141.

17. Mark Grimsley, " 'Rebels' and 'Redskins,' " in *Civilians in the Path of War*, eds. Mark Grimsley and Cliford J. Rogers (Lincoln: University of Nebraska Press, 2002), 150-151.

18. E. Susan Barber and Charles F. Ritter, "Rape," in *Women in the American Civil War*, ed. Lisa Tendrich Frank (Santa Barbara, CA: ABC-CLIO, 2008), 467-468; and E. Susan Barber and Charles F. Ritter, " 'Physical Abuse... and Rough Handling': Race, Gender, and Sexual Justice in the Occupied South," in *Occupied Women: Gender, Military Occupation, and the American Civil War*, eds. LeeAnn Whites and Alecia P. Long (Baton Rouge: Louisiana State University, 2009), 49-64.

19. Brownmiller, 163.

20. Mary R. Block, " 'An Accusation Easily to Be Made': A History of Rape Law in the Nineteenth-Century State Appellate Courts, 1800–1870," Master's thesis, University of Louisville, 1992, 35.

21. Ibid., 88.

22. Linda A. Fairstein, *Sexual Violence: Our War Against Rape* (New York: William Morrow), 1993.

23. Block, 82.

24. Charles F. Nemeth, "Character Evidence in Rape Trials in Nineteenth Century New York: Chastity and the Admissibility of Specific Acts," *Women's Rights Law Reporter* 6 (1980): 218.

25. Martin L. Lalumiere, Grant T. Harris, Vernon L. Quinsey, and Mamie E. Rice, *The Causes of Rape: Understanding Individual Differences in Male Propensity for Sexual Aggression* (Washington, DC: American Psychological Association, 2005), 25.

26. Joshua S. Goldstein, *War and Gender: How Gender Shapes the War System and Vice Versa* (Cambridge: Cambridge University Press, 2001), 368.

27. Peggy Reeves Sanday, "The Socio-Cultural Context of Rape: A Cross Cultural Study," *Journal of Social Issues* 37 (1981): 5-26.

28. Emma Holmes, *The Diary of Miss Emma Holmes: 1861–1866*, ed. John F. Marszalek (Baton Rouge: Louisiana State University Press, 1979), 430.

29. "Black Soldiers in the Civil War," National Archives, http://www.archives.gov/education/lessons/blacks-civil-war/

Chapter One

1. Matthew Hale et al., *The History of the Pleas of the Crown*, 2 vols. (1736; rpt. Robert E. Small, 1847), I, 634.

2. Barbara S. Lindemann, " 'To Ravish and Carnally Know': Rape in Eighteenth-Century Massachusetts," *Signs* 10 (Autumn 1984): 63-82.

3. Jack Marietta and G.S. Rowe, in "Rape, Law, Courts, and Customs in Pennsylvania, 1682-1800," *Sex without Consent: Rape and Sexual Coercion in America,* ed. Merril D. Smith (New York: New York University, 2001): 81-102.

4. For an in-depth analysis of rape in colonial America see Sharon Block, *Rape and Sexual Power in Early America* (Chapel Hill: University of North Carolina Press, 2006).

5. William Blackstone, *Commentaries on the Laws of England,* 4 vols. (1765-1769; rpt. Chicago, 1979), IV, 210-214 .

6. *Commonwealth v. Thomas*, 3 Va. 307 (1812).

7. Sharon Block, 151-152.

8. *United States v. Patrick*, 27 F. Cas. (District of Columbia) 460 (1812).

9. Thomas D. Morris, *Southern Slavery and the Law, 1619–1860* (Chapel Hill: University of North Carolina Press, 1996), 310.

10. Sharon Block, 171.

11. *State v. Bender,* 1 Del. Cas. 278 (1793).

12. Mary R. Block, 43.

13. *State v. Sam*, 60 N.C. 300 (1864).

14. According to M. Block, the states that did not require proof of ejaculation, only penetration, were Alabama, Kentucky, Illinois, Indiana, Pennsylvania, Tennessee, South Carolina, and Virginia.

15. In many eighteenth- and nineteenth-century civilian court transcripts, witnesses and judges were often referred to by their titles and surnames without listing their given names.

16. *State v. Wesley Gray,* 53 N.C. 170 (1860).

17. *William Blackburn v. State,* 22 Ohio St. 102 (1871).

18. Mary R. Block, 35.

19. *Pollard v. State,* 2 Iowa 567 (1856).

20. *Croghan v. State,* 22 Wis. 444 (1868).

21. "Tragedy in Alabama—Officer Killed," *Richmond Daily Dispatch,* November 13, 1863.

22. *Richmond Daily Dispatch,* April 14 and April 26, 1864.

23. Theodoric Romeyn Beck, *Elements of Medical Jurisprudence,* 2 vols. (Albany, NY: 1823), I, 83-84, and (Philadelphia: Thomas Cowperthwait, 1838), 146-147.

24. "Prosecutrix" refers to a female victim of a crime on whose behalf the state is prosecuting a suspect.

25. *State v. Tomlinson,* 11 Iowa 401 (1861).

26. Amos Dean, *Principles of Medical Jurisprudence: Designed for the Professions of Law and Medicine* (Albany, 1854), 30.

27. *State v. Hartigan,* 32 Vt. 607 (1860).

28. *People v. Hulse,* 3 Hill (N.Y.) 309 (1842).

29. *State v. Blake,* 39 Me. 322 (1855).

30. *People v. Benson,* 6 Cal. 221 (1856).

31. Nemeth, 218.

32. *People v. Abbot,* 19 Wend. (N.Y.) 192 (1838).

33. *Camp v. State,* 3 Ga. 417 (1847).

34. "Released from Prison," *Richmond Daily Dispatch,* May 30, 1861.

Chapter Two

1. D. Bacon, ed., *The New York Judicial Repository,* 6 vols. (New York: Gould and Banks, 1818–1819), I, IV, 165-173.

2. Arthur F. Howington III, "The Treatment of Slaves and Free Blacks in the State and Local Courts of Tennessee," Doctoral dissertation, Vanderbilt University, 1982, 114.

3. Sharon Block, 65.

4. *Grandison v. State,* 21 Tenn 451 (1841).

5. *Pleasant v. State,* 13 Ark 360 (1853).

6. Judith Kelleher Schafer, "The Long Arm of the Law: Slave Criminals and the Supreme Court in Antebellum Louisiana," *Tulane Law Review* 60 (June 1986): 1247-68.

7. Brackets were in transcript.

8. *George v. State,* 37 Miss. 316 (1859).

9. Diane Miller Sommerville, *Rape & Race in the Nineteenth-Century South* (Chapel Hill: University of North Carolina Press, 2004), 68.

10. "Condemned to Death," *Richmond Daily Dispatch,* August 26, 1861; and "Execution," *Richmond Daily Dispatch,* October 7, 1861.

11. "Terrible Affair in Franklin County, Ky.," *Richmond Daily Dispatch*, January 21, 1862.

12. *Commonwealth v Fields*, 31 Va. 648 (1832).

13. Sommerville, 45.

14. *State v. Sam*, 60 N.C. 300 (1864).

15. *State v. Jim*, 48 N.C. 348 (1856).

16. *State v. Peter*, 14 La. Ann. 521 (1859).

17. *State v. Peter*, 53 N.C. 19 (1860).

18. *Cato v. State*, 9 Fla. 163 (1860).

19. *Stephen v. State*, 11 Ga. 225 (1852).

20. Sommerville, 127.

21. "Negroes Condemned to be Hung," *Richmond Daily Dispatch*, July 17, 1862.

22. Brownmiller, 40.

23. Todd Salzman," 'Rape Camps,' Forced Impregnation, and Ethic Religious Cleansing: Cultural and Ethical Responses to Rape Victims in the Former Yugoslavia," in *War's Dirty Secret: Rape, Prostitution, and Other Crimes against Women*, ed. Anne Llewellyn Barstow (Cleveland, Ohio: Pilgrim Press, 2000), 81.

24. Mary Beth Norton, *Liberty's Daughters: The Revolutionary Experience of American Women, 1750–1800* (Ithaca, NY: Cornell University Press, 1995), 203.

25. Lord Francis Rawdon to Francis, tenth Earl of Huntingdon, August 5, 1776, in *The Spirit of 'Seventy-Six: The Story of the American Revolution as Told by Participants*, eds. Henry Steele Commager and Richard B. Morris (New York: Harper & Row, 1967), 424.

26. Arnold J. Toynbee, *The German Terror in Belgium: An Historical Record* (New York: George H. Doran, 1917), 91; and Arnold J. Toynbee, *The German Terror in France: An Historical Record* (New York: George H. Doran, 1917), 58, 92, 144, and 220.

27. J.H. Morgan, *German Atrocities: An Official Investigation* (New York: E.P. Dutton, 1916), 82-83.

28. George S. Patton, *War as I Knew It* (Boston: Houghton Mifflin, 1947), 23-24.

29. J. Robert Lilly, *Taken by Force: Rape and American GIs in Europe during World War II* (New York: Palgrave Macmillan, 2007), 16.

30. Lilly, 83.

31. Lilly, 107.

32. Lilly, 121.

33. United States War Department, *Official Records of the Union and Confederate Armies*, ser. 1, vol. 20, pt. 2 (Washington DC, 1880-1901), 318. Hereafter cited as *OR*.

Chapter Three

1. Lilly, 11.

2. Catherine Ann Devereux Edmonston, *Journal of a Secesh Lady: The Diary of Catherine Ann Devereux Edmonston, 1860–1866*, eds. Beth G. Crabtree and James W. Patton (Raleigh: North Carolina Division of Archives and History, 1979), 589.

3. Holmes, 384.

4. Mary Ann Jones, *Yankees a'Coming: One Month's Experience during the Invasion of Liberty County, Georgia, 1864–1865*, ed. Haskell Monroe (Tuscaloosa, AL: Confederate Press, 1959), 52.

5. Roxanna Cole, "Letter from Roxanna Cole to Blanche Underhill, November 2, 1862," in *Echoes of Happy Valley: Letters and Diaries, Family Life in the South, Civil War History*, ed. Thomas Felix Hickerson (Chapel Hill, NC: Bull's Head Bookshop, 1962), 69.

6. "The Cowardly Despotism at Washington," *Richmond Daily Dispatch*, December 11, 1861.

7. George Augustus Sala, *My Diary in America in the Midst of War* (London: Tinsley Brothers, 1865), 19.

8. Green Berry Samuels, *A Civil War Marriage in Virginia: Reminiscences and Letters*, eds. Carrie Esther Spencer, Bernard Samuels, and Walter Berry Samuels (Boyce, VA: Carr Publishing, 1956), 190.

9. "From Northern Virginia," *Richmond Daily Dispatch*, August 24, 1863.

10. John Beauchamp Jones, *A Rebel War Clerk's Diary at the Confederate States Capital*, vol. 2. (Philadelphia: J.B. Lippincott, 1866), 35.

11. National Archives, RG 153, file OO 175.

12. *OR*, series 1, vol. 15, 426.

13. *OR*, series 1, vol. 12, part 1, 51.

14. *OR*, series 1, vol. 47, part 3, 48.

15. *OR*, series 1, vol. 50, part 1, 8.

16. *OR*, series 1, vol. 51, part 2, 261.

17. *OR*, series 1, vol. 12, part 3, 196.

18. *OR*, series 1, vol. 41, part 2, 387.

19. *OR*, series 1, vol. 16, part 2, 273-275.

20. George C. Bradley and Richard L. Dahlen, *From Conciliation to Conquest: The Sack of Athens and the Court-Martial of Colonel John B. Turchin* (Tuscaloosa: University of Alabama Press, 2006), 270.

21. *OR*, Series 1, vol. 10, part 2, 204.

22. "Charges against Mitchel," *Press* (PA), July 23, 1862.

23. "Sissy" was a term meaning sister.

24. National Archives RG 153, file KK 122.

25. Bradley and Dahlen, 270.

26. "Some Thoughts about the Army," *New York Times*, September 13, 1863.

27. John Haley papers, December 10, 1864, diary entry, Dyer Library Archives and Special Collections, Saco Maine.

28. Sgt. Edwin H. Fay, *"This Infernal War": The Confederate Letters of Sgt. Ewin H. Fay*, ed. Bell Irvin Wiley (Austin: University of Texas Press, 1958), 302.

29. Teamsters drove teams of horses, mules, or oxen for a living.

30. *Arkansas True Democrat*, April 15 and May 6, 1863.

31. "A Hellish Outrage by Yankees," *Macon Daily Telegraph*, August 19, 1863.

32. "A Most Horrible Outrage by the Enemy," *Charleston Mercury*, June 17, 1864. Also in *Daily Constitutionalist* (Augusta, GA), June 19, 1864.

33. "A Fiend to Be Tried—The McNeil Murder," *Richmond Daily Dispatch*, October 10, 1863.

34. National Archives RG 153, WW 2169.

35. "The Missouri Execution Again," *New York Times*, December 4, 1862.

36. National Archives RG 153, WW 2169.

37. "Genuine Romance in Real Life," *Missouri Democrat*, September 1, 1863.

38. *Tuscaloosa Observer*, October 2, 1861.

39. "The Villainies in Maryland," *Richmond Daily Dispatch*, September 28, 1861.

40. W. Robert Beckman, "Daniel Edgar Sickles," in *Encyclopedia of the American Civil War: A Political, Social, and Military History*, eds. David S. Heidler and Jeanne T. Heidler (New York: W. W. Norton, 2000), 1784.

41. "Infamous Outrages on the Peninsula," *Richmond Daily Dispatch*, April 26, 1862.

42. Ibid.

43. "Outrages of the Enemy in Fauquier," *Richmond Daily Dispatch*, April 23, 1862; and *Macon Daily Telgraph*, April 26, 1862.

44. Robert Hale Strong, *A Yankee Private's Civil War*, ed. Ashley Halsey (Chicago: Henry Regnery, 1961), 45-46; Samuel Merrill, *The Seventieth Indi-*

ana Volunteer Infantry in the War of the Rebellion (Indianapolis: Bowen-Merrill, 1900), 227-228; and Oscar L. Jackson, *The Colonel's Diary: Journals Kept before and during the Civil War by the Late Colonel Oscar L. Jackson... Sometime Commander of the 63rd Regiment O.V.I,* 1922, 191.

45. "Movements of the Enemy Near Holly Springs," *Memphis Daily Appeal* (Grenada, MS), July 9, 1862.

46. *Charleston Mercury,* August 2, 1864.

47. "A Fiendish Outrage," *Galveston Weekly News,* September 28, 1864.

48. "Letter from North Georgia," *Charleston Mercury,* November 4, 1864.

49. *Richmond Whig,* December 7, 1864; "Sherman at Clinton," *New York Times,* December 13, 1864; and "The Nice Ladies of Milledgeville," *New York Times,* December 18, 1864.

50. Henry Hitchcock, *Marching with Sherman: Passages from the Letters and Campaign Diaries of Henry Hitchcock, Major and Assistant Adjutant General of the Volunteers, November 1864—May 1865,* ed. M.A. DeWolfe Howe (New Haven: Yale University Press, 1927), 158.

51. "The Conduct of Our Troops," *New York Times,* December 20, 1864.

52. National Archives, RG 153, MM 3937.

53. Rod Gragg, *The Illustrated Confederate Reader* (New York: Harper & Row, 1989), 192.

Chapter Four

1. National Archives RG 153, files NN 2168 and NN 3232; CMSRs Privates Lewis Hardin, George Nelson, and Daniel Tierce, M 1821.

2. National Archives RG 153, files MM 1972, MM 2006, and MM 1984.

3. National Archives RG 153, file MM 1470.

4. "Execution of the Negro Johnson," and "Petersburg Bombarded by Gen. Birney—Execution of a Negro for an Outrage upon a White Woman," *New York Times,* June 23, 1864; "The Operations of Friday, Saturday and Sunday—Our Losses, &c," *New York Times,* June 22, 1864; "Additional Details of the Siege," *Press* (PA), June 22, 1864; and Mason Whiting Tyler, *Recollections of the Civil War: with Many Original Diary Entries and Letters Written from the Seat of War, and with Annotated References,* ed. William S. Tyler (New York: G.P. Putnam's Sons, 1912), 230.

5. National Archives RG 153, file MM 3184.

6. National Archives RG 153, file MM 3197.

7. A drumhead court-martial was a less formal court-martial held in the field. Punishments were generally carried out shortly after sentencing.

8. National Archives Microfilm, M1818; and *OR*, Series I, Vol. 49, Part 2, 669-670.

9. The previous year, Smith had been returned to duty after desertion.

10. National Archives Microfilm, M1801; "Military Executions," *Press* (PA), March 2, 1864; and "Wholesome Hanging at Jacksonville," *New York Herald*, March 2, 1864.

11. National Archives Microfilm, M2000.

12. National Archives CMSR Private Henry Jay.

13. Robert I. Alotta, *Civil War Justice: Union Army Executions under Lincoln* (Shippenburg, PA: White Mane, 1989), 187.

Chapter Five

1. National Archives CMSR Private John Bell; and "From the Second Regiment," *Daily Times* (Leavenworth, KS), July 26, 1862.

2. William Corby, *Memoirs of Chaplain Life: Three Years Chaplain in the Famous Irish Brigade, "Army of the Potomac"* (Chicago: Le Monte, O'Donnell, 1893), 223.

3. National Archives RG 153, file MM 792.

4. Corby, 221-228.

5. John G. B. Adams, *Reminiscences of the Nineteenth Massachusetts Regiment* (Boston: Wright & Potter, 1899), 84-86.

6. National Archives RG 153, file NN 1740; and CMSR Private John Callaghan (Callaghan was spelled with a "g" in the CMSR and without in the court-martial transcript).

7. National Archives RG 153, file MM 1372; and CMSR Private John Carrol (Carroll was spelled Carrol in the CMSR and Carroll in the court-martial transcript).

8. National Archives RG 153, files NN 2427 and NN 2998; and CMSR Sergeant Charles Sperry.

9. National Archives RG 153, file MM 1481.

10. Burke Davis, *The Civil War: Strange and Fascinating Facts* (New York: Wings Books, 1982), 160.

11. "The War," *Press* (PA), July 19, 1864.

12. Marsena Rudolph Patrick, Journal, 1862–1865, Library of Congress, Washington, D.C.

13. Corby, 247.

14. *Press* (PA), July 19, 1864.

15. National Archives CMSR Private Daniel Geary.

16. "Two Soldiers Hanged for Rape," *Newark Advocate* (OH), August 19, 1864.

17. Patrick, Journal.

18. National Archives RG 153, file MM 1774; and William Bircher, *A Drummer-Boy's Diary: Comprising Four Years of Service with the Second Regiment Minnesota Veteran Volunteers, 1861 to 1865* (St. Paul, MN: St. Paul Book and Stationery, 1889), 176-180.

19. National Archives RG 153, file MM 3032; and CMSR Private John Vincent.

20. Alotta, 187.

Chapter Six

1. OR, ser. 3, vol. 4, 1029.

2. J.S. McCulloch, *Reminiscences of Life in the Army and as a Prisoner of War*, photocopy transcript 1910, www.archives.org, 6.

3. "From Gen. Lee's Army," *Richmond Daily Dispatch*, December 8, 1863; and "The Movements on the Peninsula," *Richmond Daily Dispatch*, May 7, 1864.

4. "Villainous Conduct of a Massachusetts Officer," *Republican Compiler* (PA), August 22, 1864.

5. "Terrible Revenge," *Chicago Tribune*, March 28, 1865.

6. "Peninsular Affairs," *Yorktown Cavalier* (VA), October 12, 1863.

7. National Archives RG 153, file NN 375; and CMSR Private Patrick Tully.

8. National Archives RG 153, file LL 3201; CMSR Private William Hilton; and OR Series 1, Vol. 41, Part 1, 928.

9. National Archives RG 153, file NN 2099.

10. "Punishment of a Military Criminal," *New York Times*, August 2, 1864.

11. National Archives RG 153, file NN 2099.

12. Abraham Lincoln, *The Collected Works of Abraham Lincoln*, ed. Roy P. Basler (New Brunswick, NJ: Rutgers University, 1953), Vol. 8, 193.

13. National Archives RG 153, file OO 654; and CMSRs Privates Charles Clark and Joseph Redmond.

14. National Archives RG 153, file MM 2471; and CMSRs Privates Thomas Killgore and David Kunkle.

15. National Archives RG 153, file NN 624.

16. National Archives RG 153, file MM 2806.

17. National Archives RG 153, file NN 3743; and CMSR Corporal George Hakes.

18. National Archives RG 153, file MM 1909.

19. National Archives RG 153, file OO 886; and CMSR Private Thomas Mitchell, microfilm M 2004.

20. National Archives RG 153, file MM 746; and CMSR Private Perry Pierson.

21. National Archives RG 153, file LL 380.

22. National Archives RG 153, file KK 207; and CMSRs Privates Louis Sorg and Lewis Trost.

23. National Archives RG 153, file LL 3253; and CMSRs Privates James Deery and Augustine Morrison, microfilm M 396.

24. National Archives RG 153, file LL 2755.

25. National Archives RG 153, file NN 2140.

26. National Archives RG 153, file LL 192; and CMSR William C. Chinock.

27. National Archives RG 153, file OO 927; and CMSRs Lieutenant Dudley O. Bravard and Private John Linville, microfilm M 397.

28. National Archives RG 153, file LL 298; and CMSR Henry Murphy.

29. Most commissioned officers of black troops were white.

30. National Archives RG 153, files MM 3318 and MM 2780; and CMSR Lieutenant Charles Wenz, microfilm M1817.

31. National Archives RG 153, file MM 3169.

32. National Archives RG 153, file MM 3937.

33. National Archives RG 153, files NN 2812, LL 2193, and LL 2227.

Chapter Seven

1. Joseph Addison Waddell, Diary, 1855-1865, University of Virginia collection; and Clara D. Maclean, "The Last Raid," *Southern Historical Society Papers* 13 (1885): 471-72.

2. *Richmond Daily Dispatch*, July 24, 1863; and John McGill, "The War Letters of the Bishop of Richmond," ed. Willard E. Wright, *Virginia Magazine of History and Biography* 67 (July 1959): 265.

3. *Richmond Daily Dispatch*, December 1, 1862, June 20 and 24, 1863.

4. Holmes, 79-80; *New York Times*, May 27, 1861; and "Later from Alexandria," *Semi-Weekly Raleigh Register*, June 5, 1861.

5. "Charged with Rape," *Macon Telegraph*, May 14, 1863; and National Archives CMSR Robert Christian.

6. *Daily Times* (Leavenworth, KS), June 15, 1862.

7. *Arkansas True Democrat*, October 1, 1862.

8. *OR*, Series 1, Vol. 27, Part 2, 983; and CMSR Private James H. Curham.

9. *OR*, Series 1, Vol 47, Part 3, 79.

10. National Archives RG 153 file, NN 3205

11. National Archives RG 153 file, KK 76.

12. National Archives RG 153 file, OO 1017; and CMSRs Privates Francis Enger and Joseph Holroyed, microfilm M 396.

13. National Archives RG 153, file NN 2165.

14. William R. Hartpence, *History of the Fifty-First Indiana Veteran Volunteer Infantry* (Harrison, Ohio: published by author, 1894), 227; and "Our Indianapolis Letter," *Chicago Tribune*, December 28, 1864.

15. National Archives RG 153, file NN 751.

16. National Archives, RG 153, file LL 1097.

17. National Archives, RG 153, file MM 2547.

18. National Archives, RG 153, file NN 192; and CMSR Private Charles Hunter, microfilm M 397.

19. National Archives, RG 153, file MM 742; and CMSR Lieutenant Harvey John.

20. National Archives, RG 153, file OO 1320; and CMSR Private Michael Shean. (Shehan was spelled without an "h" in the CMSR and with in the court-martial transcripts.)

21. National Archives, RG 153, file NN 2227; and CMSRs Corporal Jacob Blatner and Private John Williams, microfilm M 508. (Bladner was spelled Blatner in the CMSR.)

22. National Archives, RG 153, files LL 3132 and NN 2113; and CMSRs Privates William Jones and Horace Ralph.

23. National Archives, RG 153, file NN 3927; and CMSR Private Thomas Bond.

24. National Archives, RG 153, file MM 402; and CMSR Lieutenant George O'Malley.

25. National Archives, RG 153, file OO 1416; and CMSR Evan Williams.

26. National Archives, RG 153, file MM 1170; and CMSR Perry Holland.

27. National Archives, RG 153, file NN 3857.

28. National Archives, RG 153, file MM 1054.

29. National Archives, RG 153, file OO 945; and CMSR John W. Dodge.

30. National Archives, RG 153, file NN 2919; and CMSR Charles Helton microfilm M 397.

31. National Archives, RG 153, file NN 3809.

Chapter Eight

1. Nicola Henry et al., "A Multifactorial Model of Wartime Rape," *Aggression and Violent Behavior* 9, no. 5 (2004): 535-562; and Lisa S. Price, "Finding the Man in the Soldier-Rapist: Some Reflections on Comprehension and Accountability," *Women's Studies International Forum* 24, no 2 (2001): 211-227.

2. National Archives RG 153, files LL 2552 and NN 2468.

3. National Archives RG 153, file LL 3253; and CMSRs Privates Joshua Childers, Mark Tulley, Lewis Sappington, and George R. Hoopengarner.

4. National Archives RG 153, files MM 2571 and OO 1319; and "Political Items," *Erie Observer*, September 14, 1865.

5. National Archives RG 153, file II 999.

6. "From Reverend George Whipple," *American Missionary*, September 1862, 208.

7. Holmes, 430.

8. McCarter, Journal, 1860–1866, Library of Congress, 85.

9. Gragg, 192; and William Gilmore Simms, *Sack and Destruction of the City of Columbia, S.C.*, ed. A.S. Salley (Atlanta: Oglethorpe University Press, 1937), 55.

10. "The Yankee Outrages in Tennessee," *Richmond Daily Dispatch*, March 12, 1863; "Horrors of War," *Republican Compiler* (PA), September 5, 1864; and *OR*, Series I, Vol. 40, Part 3, 743.

11. Céline Frémaux Garcia, *Celine: Remembering Louisiana, 1850–1871*, ed. Patrick J. Geary (Athens: University of Georgia Press, 1987), 111-112.

12. William Beverley Pettit papers, Arabella Speairs Pettit to husband, October 1, 1863, University of North Carolina collection.

13. *Savannah Republican* (GA), May 2, 1862; and *OR*, Series I, Vol. 15, 373.

14. "The Stoneman Raid," *Charleston Mercury*, August 10, 1864.

15. Governor Henry W. Allen, *Official Report Relative to the Conduct of Federal Troops in Western Louisiana, During the Invasions of 1863 and 1864*, Shreveport, Louisiana, 1865.

16. "Shocking Affair, Women Tortured, Robbery, Murder & Arson, A 'Reverend' in Irons, etc, etc.," *Fort Smith New Era* (AR), February 11, 1865; and "More Prisoners from Clarksville," *National Democrat* (Little Rock, AR), February 25, 1865.

17. "Corruption and Villainy Unparalleled," *National Democrat* (Little Rock, AR), April 1, 1865.

18. National Archives CMSRs Privates Calvin Asberry Allison, Robert Atwell, William B. Farmer, Henry Lowery, Edward Rucker, Gaines Simco, Sergeants Wisner Condra, John Buckhanan Mills, Adam Patrick Scott, and Lieutenant Charles O. Kimball.

19. *OR*, Series I, Vol. 49, Part 2, 427; and National Archives CMSR Private Thomas H. Brewer, microfilm M 395.

20. *OR*, Series I, Vol. 3, 459; Vol. 16, Part 2, 319; and Vol. 40, Part 2, 705.

21. "Correspondence of the Richmond Dispatch," *Richmond Daily Dispatch,* January 21, 1862; and "Fiends in Human Shape," *Memphis Daily Appeal*, February 21, 1862.

22. "Federal Outrages in Arkansas," *Savannah Republican* (GA), August 9, 1862; and "Fiendish Outrage," *True Democrat* (AR), December 24, 1862.

23. "The Raiders that Came to Richmond," *Richmond Daily Dispatch*, May 17, 1864; and "Yankee Atrocities," *Memphis Daily Appeal*, June 27, 1864.

24. "Murder of Negro Troops Admitted," *New York Times*, July 12, 1864.

25. *OR*, Series I, Vol. 13, 769; and "Interesting Federal Reports from Arkansas," *Memphis Daily Appeal*, November 11, 1862.

Chapter Nine

1. National Archives RG 153, file MM 2802; and Stephen S. Michot, " 'War Is Still Raging in This Part of the Country': Oath-Taking, Consription, and Guerrilla War in Louisiana's Lafourche Region," *Louisiana History: The Journal of the Louisiana Historical Association* 38, no 2 (Spring 1997): 183.

2. *OR*, Series I, Vol. 49, Part 2, 737.

3. National Archives RG 153, file MM 2900.

4. National Archives RG 153, file MM 3553.

5. Thomas Berry, *Four Years with Morgan and Forrest* (Oklahoma City: Harlowe-Ratcliff, 1914), 100-101; National Archives RG 153, file MM 3528; and Thomas Shelby Watson and Perry A. Brantley, *Confederate Guerrilla Sue Mundy: A Biography of Kentucky Soldier Jerome Clarke* (Jefferson, NC: McFarland, 2008), 196-199.

6. Watson and Brantley, 33-34; and National Archives RG 153, file MM 2958.

7. Massachusetts Executive Office of Public Safety and Security, *Adult Sexual Assault Law Enforcement Guidelines* (Boston, 2009), 14; and Oregon Criminal

Justice Committee, Attorney General's Sexual Assault Task Force, *False Allegations, Case Unfounding and Victim Recantations in the Context of Sexual Assault* (Eugene, 2008), 1-3.

8. Watson and Brantley, 216; and "The Execution of the Guerrilla Magruder," *Daily Evening Bulletin* (PA), October 25, 1865.

9. John M. Palmer, *Personal Recollections of John M. Palmer: The Story of an Earnest Life* (Cincinnati: Robert Clark, 1901), 268-269; John N. Edwards, *Noted Guerrillas of the Border: Guerrillas of the West* (St. Louis: Bryan, Brand, 1877), 443-446; Watson and Brantley, 189-191; and National Archives RG 153, file MM 3528 (testimony by C.J. Wilson, Major General John Palmer, and Thomas Kirk in the trial of Samuel O. Berry).

10. National Archives RG 153, file MM 1021.

11. National Archives, RG 109, Chapter 1, Volume 3, 252.

12. "Three Union Ladies Violated," *Chicago Tribune*, October 13, 1862; "Brutal Outrage—Three Union Ladies Violated," *Altoona Tribune* (PA), October 16, 1862; and *Nashville Daily Union*, October 4, 1862.

13. "The Invasion," *Press* (PA), July 2, 1863; and "The Rebel Invasion," *Press* (PA), August 6, 1864.

14. "Police Court, July 16th," *Richmond Daily Dispatch*, July 17, 1862; "Hustings Court, March 11," *Richmond Daily Dispatch*, March 13, 1862; and "City Intelligence," *Richmond Examiner*, June 13, 18, and 26, 1862.

15. "[Special Correspondence of the Dispatch.],"*Richmond Daily Dispatch*, November 5, 1861; and " 'Bray a Fool in Mortar,' &c.," *Richmond Daily Dispatch*, November 11, 1861.

16. *OR*, series I, vol. 29, part 1, 946.

17. *Agitator* (PA), February 5, 1862; and "Rebel Outrage," *Rolla Express* (MO), August 30, 1862.

18. "Chattanooga," *Vicksburg Daily Herald* (MS), March 25, 1865.

19. George L. Griscom, *Fighting with Ross' Texas Cavalry Brigade C.S.A.: The Diary of George L. Griscom, Adjutant, 9th Texas Cavalry*, ed. Homer L. Kerr (Hillsboro, TX: Hill Jr. College Press, 1976), 3; and "A Spy Hung in Texas," *Richmond Daily Dispatch*, December 2, 1861.

20. *OR*, Series I, Vol. 32, Part 3, 625.

21. "From Lamine Bridge," *Missouri Democrat*, October 24, 1864; "From Kansas City," *Chicago Tribune*, October 25, 1864; and "Outrage on Two Negro Women," *New York Times*, November 20, 1864.

22. Louis F. Kakuske, *A Civil War Drama: The Adventures of a Union Soldier in Southern Imprisonment*, trans. from the original German by Herbert P. Kakuske (New York: Carlton Press, 1970), 40-41.

Conclusion

1. National Archives RG 153, file MM 0660; and CMSR Private Eden Hill, microfilm M405.

2. National Archives RG 153, file MM 2407.

Bibliography

Books

Secondary Sources

Alotta, Robert I. *Civil War Justice: Union Army Executions under Lincoln.* Shippensburg, PA: White Mane Publishing, 1989.

Ash, Stephen V. *When the Yankees Came: Conflict and Chaos in the Occupied South, 1861–1865.* Chapel Hill: University of North Carolina Press, 1995.

Barber, E. Susan and Charles F. Ritter. "Rape," in *Women in the American Civil War,* ed. Lisa Tendrich Frank. Santa Barbara, CA: ABC-CLIO, 2008.

———. " 'Physical Abuse ... and Rough Handling' Race, Gender, and Sexual Justice in the Occupied South," in *Occupied Women: Gender, Military Occupation, and the American Civil War,* eds. LeeAnn Whites and Alecia P. Long. Baton Rouge: Louisiana State University, 2009.

Beattie, J.M. *Crime and the Courts in England, 1660–1800.* Oxford: Clarendon Press, 1986.

Beckman, David S. "Daniel Edgar Sickles," in *Encyclopedia of the American Civil War,* eds. David S. Heidler and Jeanne T. Heidler. New York: W.W. Norton, 2000.

Berlin, Ira. *The Wartime Genesis of Free Labor: The Lower South.* Cambridge: Cambridge University Press, 1990.

Blanton, DeAnne, and Lauren M. Cook. *They Fought Like Demons: Women Soldiers in the Civil War.* New York: Vintage Books, 2002.

Block, Sharon. *Rape and Sexual Power in Early America.* Chapel Hill: University of North Carolina Press, 2006.

Bradley, George C., and Richard L. Dahlen. *From Conciliation to Conquest: The Sack of Athens and the Court-Martial of Colonel John B. Turchin.* Tuscaloosa: University of Alabama Press, 2006.

Brownmiller, Susan. *Against Our Will: Men, Women, and Rape.* New York: Simon and Schuster, 1975.

Clinton, Catherine. *Tara Revisited: Women, War, and the Plantation Legend.* New York: Abbeville Press, 1995.

Davis, Burke. *The Civil War: Strange and Fascinating Facts.* New York: Wings Books, 1982, 1960.

Engs, Robert Francis. *Freedom's First Generation: Black Hampton, Virginia, 1861–1890.* Philadelphia: University of Pennsylvania Press, 1979.

Fairstein, Linda A. *Sexual Violence: Our War against Rape.* New York: William Morrow, 1993.

Frederick, Sharon, and the Aware Committee on Rape. *Rape: Weapon of Terror.* River Edge, NJ: Global Publishing, 2001.

Fellman, Michael. *Inside War: The Guerrilla Conflict in Missouri During the American Civil War.* New York: Oxford University Press, 1989.

Glatthaar, Joseph T. *The March to the Sea and Beyond: Sherman's Troops in the Savannah and Carolinas Campaigns.* New York: New York University Press, 1985.

——. *Forged in Battle: The Civil War Alliance of Black Soldiers and White Officers.* New York: Free Press, 1990.

Goldstein, Joshua S. *War and Gender: How Gender Shapes the War System and Vice Versa.* Cambridge: Cambridge University Press, 2001.

Gragg, Rod. *The Illustrated Confederate Reader.* New York: Harper & Row, 1989.

Grimsley, Mark. *The Hard Hand of War: Union Military Policy Toward Southern Civilians, 1861–1865.* Cambridge: Cambridge University Press, 1995.

——. " 'Rebels' and 'Redskins,' " in *Civilians in the Path of War,* eds. Mark Grimsley and Cliford J. Rogers. Lincoln: University of Nebraska Press, 2002.

Hodes, Martha. *White Women, Black Men: Illicit Sex in the Nineteenth-Century South.* New Haven: Yale University Press, 1997.

Jordan, Ervin L., Jr. *Black Confederates and Afro-Yankees in Civil War Virginia.* Charlottesville: University Press of Virginia, 1995.

——. "Mirrors beyond Memories: Afro-Virginians and the Civil War," in *New Perspectives on the Civil War: Myths and Realities of the National Conflict.* Madison, WI: Madison House Publishers, 1998.

Lalumiere, Martin L., Grant T. Harris, Vernon L. Quinsey, and Marnie E. Rice. *The Causes of Rape: Understanding Individual Differences in Male Propensity for Sexual Aggression*. Washington, DC: American Psychological Association, 2005.

Leslie, Edward E. *The Devil Knows How to Ride*. New York: Random House, 1996.

Lily, J. Robert. *Taken by Force: Rape and American GIs in Europe during World War II*. New York: Pelgrave MacMillan, 2007.

Marietta, Jack and G.S. Rowe. "Rape, Law Courts, and Customs in Pennsylvania, 1682-1800," in *Sex Without Consent: Rape and Sexual Coercion in America*, ed. Merril D. Smith. New York: New York University, 2001.

Mitchell, Reid. *The Vacant Chair: The Northern Soldier Leaves Home*. New York: Oxford University Press, 1993.

Morris, Thomas D. *Southern Slavery and the Law, 1619–1860*. Chapel Hill: North Carolina Press, 1996.

Norton, Mary Beth. *Liberty's Daughters: The Revolutionary Experience of American Women, 1750–1800*. Ithaca, NY: Cornell University Press, 1996.

Rable, George C. *Civil Wars: Women and the Crisis of Southern Nationalism*. Urbana: University of Illinois Press, 1989.

Royster, Charles. *The Destructive War: William Tecumseh Sherman, Stonewall Jackson, and the Americans*. New York: Knopf, 1991.

Salzman, Todd. " 'Rape Camps,' Forced Impregnation, and Ethic Religious Cleansing: Cultural and Ethical Responses to Rape Victims in the Former Yugoslavia," in *War's Dirty Secret: Rape, Prostitution, and Other Crimes Against Women*. Cleveland, Ohio: Pilgrim Press, 2000.

Samito, Christian G. *Becoming American under Fire: Irish Americans, African Americans, and the Politics of Citizenship During the Civil War Era*. Ithaca, NY: Cornell University Press, 2009.

Sanday, Peggy Reeves. "Rape-Free versus Rape-Prone," in *Evolution, Gender, and Rape*, ed. Cheryl Brown Travis. Cambridge, MA: MIT Press, 2003.

Sickles, John. *The Legends of Sue Mundy and One Armed Berry: Confederate Guerrillas*. Merrillville, IN: Heritage Press, 1999.

Smith, Andrea. *Conquest: Sexual Violence and American Indian Genocide*. Cambridge, MA: South End Press, 2005.

Sommerville, Diane Miller. *Rape and Race in the Nineteenth-Century South*. Chapel Hill: University of North Carolina Press, 2004.

Watson, Thomas Shelby and Perry A. Brantley. *Confederate Guerrilla Sue Mundy: A Biography of Kentucky Soldier Jerome Clarke*. Jefferson, NC: McFarland, 2008.

Wylie, Bell, I. *The Life of Billy Yank, the Common Soldier of the Union*. Indianapolis: Bobbs-Merrill, 1952.

Books

Printed Primary Sources

Adams, John G. B. *Reminiscences of the Nineteenth Massachusetts Regiment*. Boston: Wright & Potter, 1899.

Allen, Governor Henry W. *Official Report Relative to the Conduct of Federal Troops in Western Louisiana, During the Invasions of 1863 and 1864*. Shreveport, Louisiana: 1865.

Bacon, D. ed. "The People v Charles Carpenter," in *The New York Judicial Repository*, 6 vols. New York: Gould and Banks, 1818-1819.

Beck, Theodoric Romeyn. *Elements of Medical Jurisprudence*. 2 vols. Albany, New York: Webster and Skinner, 1823.

Beck, Theodoric Romeyn and John B. Beck. *Elements of Medical Jurisprudence*. 2 vols. Philadelphia: Thomas Cowperthwait, 1838.

Berry, Thomas F. *Four Years with Morgan and Forrest*. Oklahoma City: Harlow-Ratcliff, 1914.

Bircher, William. *A Drummer-Boy's Diary: Comprising Four Years of Service with the Second Regiment Minnesota Veteran Volunteers, 1861 to 1865*. St. Paul, MN: St. Paul Book and Stationery, 1889.

Blackstone, William. *Commentaries on the Laws of England*, 4 vols., 1765-1769; rpt. Chicago, 1979.

Cole, Roxanna, "Letter from Roxanna Cole to Blanche Underhill, November 2, 1862," in *Echoes of Happy Valley: Letters and Diaries, Family Life in the South, Civil War History*, ed. Thomas Felix Hickerson. Chapel Hill, NC: Bull's Head Bookshop, 1962.

Corby, William. *Memoirs of Chaplain Life: Three Years Chaplain in the Famous Irish Brigade, "Army of the Potomac."* Chicago: Le Monte, O'Donnell, 1893.

Dean, Amos. *Principles of Medical Jurisprudence: Designed for the Professions of Law and Medicine*. Albany: 1854.

Edmonston, Catherine Ann Devereux. *Journal of a Secesh Lady: The Diary of Catherine Ann Devereux Edmonston, 1860–1866*, eds. Beth

G. Crabtree and James W. Patton. Raleigh: North Carolina Division of Archives and History, 1979.

Edwards, John N. *Noted Guerrillas of the Warfare of the Border: Guerrillas of the West.* St. Louis: Bryan, Brand & Company, 1877.

Fay, Sgt. Edwin H. *"This Infernal War": The Confederate Letters of Sgt. Edwin H. Fay,* ed. Bell Irvin Wiley. Austin: University of Texas Press, 1958.

Garcia, Céline Frémaux. *Celine: Remembering Louisiana, 1850–1871,* ed. Patrick J. Geary. Athens, GA: University of Georgia Press, 1987.

Garfield, James A. *The Wild Life of the Army: Civil War Letters of James A. Garfield,* ed. Frederick D. Williams. Lansing: Michigan State University Press, 1964.

Gray, John Chipman. *War Letters, 1862–1915.* Boston and New York: Houghton Mifflin, 1927.

Griscom, George L. *Fighting with Ross' Texas Cavalry Brigade C.S.A.: The Diary of George L. Griscom, Adjutant, 9th Texas Cavalry,* ed. Homer L. Kerr. Hillsboro, TX: Hill Jr. College Press, 1976.

Hale, Matthew et al. *The History of the Pleas of the Crown.* 2 vols., 1736; rpt. Robert E. Small, 1847.

Hartpence, William R. *History of the Fifty-First Indiana Veteran Volunteer Infantry: A Narrative of its Organization, Marches, Battles and Other Experiences in Camp and Prison.* Harrison, Ohio: Published by Author, 1894.

Hitchcock, Henry. *Marching with Sherman: Passages from the Letters and Campaign Diaries of Henry Hitchcock, Major and Assistant Adjutant General of the Volunteers, November 1864–May 1865,* ed. M.A. DeWolfe Howe. New Haven: Yale University Press, 1927.

Holmes, Emma. *The Diary of Miss Emma Holmes: 1861–1866,* ed. John F. Marszalek. Baton Rouge: Louisiana State University Press, 1979.

Jackson, Henry W. R. *The Southern Women of the Second American Revolution.* Atlanta: Intelligencer Steam-Power Presses, 1863.

Jackson, Oscar L. *The Colonel's Diary: Journals Kept Before and During the Civil War by the Late Colonel Oscar L. Jackson... Sometime Commander of the 63rd Regiment O.V.I,* 1922.

Jones, John Beauchamp. *A Rebel War Clerk's Diary at the Confederate States Capital.* 2 vols. Philadelphia: J.B. Lippincott, 1866.

Jones, Mary Sharpe Jones. *Yankees a' Coming: One Month's Experience During the Invasion of Liberty County, Georgia, 1864–1865,* ed. Haskell Monroe. Tuscaloosa, AL: Confederate Press, 1959.

Kakuske, Louis F. *A Civil War Drama: The Adventures of a Union Soldier in Southern Imprisonment,* trans. Herbert P. Kakuske. New York: Carlton Press, 1970.

Lincoln, Abraham. *The Collected Works of Abraham Lincoln,* ed. Roy P. Basler. 9 vols. New Brunswick, NJ: Rutgers University Press, 1953.

Merrill, Samuel. *The Seventieth Indiana Volunteer Infantry in the War of the Rebellion.* Indianapolis: Bowen-Merrill, 1900.

Morgan, J.H. *German Atrocities: An Official Investigation.* New York: E.P. Dutton, 1916.

Palmer, John M. *Personal Recollections of John M. Palmer: The Story of an Earnest Life.* Cincinnati: Robert Clarke, 1901.

Patrick, Marsena Rudolph. *Inside Lincoln's Army: The Diary of Marsena Rudolph Patrick, Provost Marshal General, Army of the Potomac,* ed. David S. Sparks. New York: Thomas Yoseloff, 1964.

Patton, George S., Jr. *War as I Knew It.* Boston: Houghton Mifflin, 1947.

Pettit, Arabella Speairs, and William Beverley Pettit. *Civil War Letters of Arabella Speairs and William Beverley Pettit of Fluvanna County, Virginia, March 1862–March 1865,* ed. Charles W. Turner. Roanoke: Virginia Lithography and Graphics, 1988.

Rawdon, Francis. *The Spirit of 'Seventy-Six: The Story of the American Revolution as Told by Participants,* eds. Henry Steele Commager and Richard B. Morris. New York: Harper & Row, 1967.

Sala, George Augustus. *My Diary in America in the Midst of War.* London: Tinsley Brothers, 1865.

Samuels, Green Berry. *A Civil War Marriage in Virginia: Reminiscences and Letters,* eds. Carrie Esther Spencer, Bernard Samuels, and Walter Berry Samuels. Boyce, VA: Carr Publishing, 1956.

Simms, William Gilmore. *Sack and Destruction of the City of Columbia, S.C.,* ed. A.S. Salley. Atlanta: Oglethorpe University Press, 1937.

Sterling, Dorothy, ed. *We Are Your Sisters: Black Women in the Nineteenth Century.* New York: W. W. Norton, 1984.

Strong, Robert Hale. *A Yankee Private's Civil War,* ed. Ashley Halsey. Chicago: Henry Regnery, 1961.

Toynbee, Arnold J. *The German Terror in Belgium: An Historical Record.* New York: George H. Doran, 1917.

———. *The German Terror in France: An Historical Record.* New York: George H. Doran, 1917.

Tyler, Mason Whiting. *Recollections of the Civil War: with Many Original Diary Entries and Letters Written from the Seat of War, and with*

Annotated References, ed. William S. Tyler. New York: G.P. Putnam's Sons, 1912.

United States Army Surgeon General's Office. *The Medical and Surgical History of the War of the Rebellion.* 6 vols. Washington, D.C., 1870–1888.

United States War Department. *Official Records of the Union and Confederate Armies.* 128 vols. Washington, D.C., 1880–1901.

Waitz, Julia Ellen LeGrand. *The Journal of Julia LeGrand: New Orleans 1862–1863,* eds. Kate Mason Rowland and Agnes E. Richmond. Croxall, VA: Everett Waddey, 1911.

Woodruff, Mathew. *A Union Soldier in the Land of the Vanquished: The Diary of Sergeant Mathew Woodruff, June–December, 1865,* ed. F.N. Boney. Birmingham: University of Alabama, 1969.

Articles, Theses, and Dissertations

Block, Mary R. " 'An Accusation Easily to be Made': A History of Rape Law in Nineteenth–Century State Appellate Courts, 1800–1870." Master's thesis, University of Louisville, 1992.

———. " 'An Accusation Easily to be Made': A History of Rape Law in Nineteenth–Century America." Doctoral dissertation, University of Kentucky, 2001.

Fellman, Michael. "Inside Wars: The Cultural Crisis of Warfare and the Values of Ordinary People." *Australasian Journal of American Studies* 10, no. 2 (December 1991).

Henry, Nicola, et al. "A Multifactorial Model of Wartime Rape." *Aggression and Violent Behavior* 9, no. 5 (2004).

Howington, Arthur F. "The Treatment of Slaves and Free Blacks in the State and Local Courts of Tennessee." Doctoral dissertation, Vanderbilt University, 1982.

Jordan, Ervin L., Jr., "Sleeping with the Enemy: Sex, Black Women, and the Civil War." *Western Journal of Black Studies* 18 (Summer 1994).

Lindemann, Barbara S. " 'To Ravish and Carnally Know': Rape in Eighteenth–Century Massachusetts." *Signs: Journal of Women in Culture and Society* 10 (Autumn 1984).

Maclean, Clara D. "The Last Raid." *Southern Historical Society Papers* 13 (1885).

Massachusetts Executive Office of Public Safety and Security. *Adult Sexual Assault Law Enforcement Guidelines*. Boston, 2009.

McGill, John. "War Letters of the Bishop of Richmond," ed. Willard E. Wright. *Virginia Magazine of History and Biography* 67, no 3. (July 1959).

Michot, Stephen S. " 'War Is Still Raging in This Part of the Country': Oath-Taking, Conscription, and Guerrilla War in Louisiana's Lafourche Region." *Louisiana History* 38, no. 2 (Spring 1997).

Nemeth, Charles F. "Character Evidence in Rape Trials in Nineteenth Century New York: Chastity and the Admissibility of Specific Acts." *Women's Rights Law Reporter* 6 (Spring 1980).

Oregon Criminal Justice Committee. Attorney General's Sexual Assault Task Force. *False Allegations, Case Unfounding and Victim Recantations in the Context of Sexual Assault*. Eugene, 2008.

Plante, Trevor K. "The Shady Side of the Family Tree: Civil War Union Court-Martial Case Files." *Prologue*. Washington, DC: National Archives and Records Administration, 1998. http://www.archives.gov/publications/prologue/1998/winter/union-court-martials.html

Price, Lisa S. "Finding the Man in the Soldier-Rapist: Some Reflections on Comprehension and Accountability." *Women's Studies International Forum* 24, no. 2 (2001).

Sanday, Peggy Reeves. "The Socio-Cultural Context of Rape: A Cross Cultural Study." *Journal of Social Issues* 37, no. 4 (1981).

Schafer, Judith Kelleher. "The Long Arm of the Law: Slave Criminals and the Supreme Court in Antebellum Louisiana." *Tulane Law Review* 10 (June 1986).

Whipple, George. "From Reverend George Whipple." *American Missionary* 6 (September 1862).

Manuscript Collections

Emmerson, Nancy. Diary. *The Valley of the Shadow*. Charlottesville: University of Virginia.

Haley, John. Diary. Saco, Maine: Dyer Library.

McCarter. Journal, 1860–1866. Washington, D.C.: Library of Congress.

McCulloch, John Scouller. *Reminiscences of Life in the Army and as a Prisoner of War*. Photocopy of typescript, 1910. http://www.archive.org/

Patrick, Marsena Rudolph. Journal, 1862–1865. Washington, D.C.: Library of Congress.

Pettit, William Beverley. Papers. Chapel Hill: University of North Carolina.

Waddell, Joseph Addison. Diary. Charlottesville: University of Virginia.

Courts-Martial

Court martial files cited are located in Record Group 153, Records of the Judge Advocate General's Office (Army) entry 15, in the National Archives and Records Administration, Washington, D.C. After the name and unit of the defendant(s), the proceeding file number is provided in parentheses.

Ayers, John H., Arthur Hinton, and Louis Knox, civilians (OO 1319)

Berry, Samuel O., John Brothers, and "Texas," Confederate (MM 3528)

Billingsly, Charles, and William Cutsinger, 7th Indiana Light Artillery (NN 2165)

Bladner, Jacob, and John Williams, 4th West Virginia Cavalry (NN 2227)

Bond, Thomas, 9th Pennsylvania Reserve Infantry (NN 3927)

Bork, Adolph, 183rd Ohio Infantry (MM 2407)

Boudreaux, Omer, Confederate (MM 2802)

Bravard, Dudley O., and John Linville, 54th Kentucky Infantry (OO 927)

Brennan, John, William Henry Cahill, Owen Curren, Thomas Hunt, Nicholas Kane, and Edward Pickett, 20th New York Cavalry (NN 2468)

Brooks, Danbridge, 38th USCT (MM 1972)

Burns, Hugh, 108th Illinois Infantry (NN 3205)

Calla(g)han, John, Thomas Johnson, and John (Jacob) Snover, 2nd New Jersey Cavalry (NN 1740)

Carroll, John, 20th Wisconsin Cavalry (MM 1372)

Childers, Josh, G. Hoopingamer, Lewis Sappington, and Mark Tulley, 52nd Indiana Infantry (LL 3253)

Chinock, William W., 26th Massachusetts Infantry (LL 192)

Clark, Charles, 20th New York Cavalry (OO 654)

Cole, William H., 109th New York Infantry (NN 751)

Corey, Robert, 56th New York Infantry (NN 2812)

Cox, Frederick, 115th Ohio Infantry (MM 2806)

Cox, Isaac, 5th U.S. Artillery (LL 2755)

Davis, Benjamin, 1st Missouri Cavalry, and William Evans, 59th Illinois Infantry (KK 76)

Davis, Henry, Howard Dixon, Gabriel Richardson, and Isau Tobey, 104th USCT (MM 3197)

Davis, John, and James Jackson, 56th New York Infantry (LL 2193)

Dawson, Thomas, 19th Massachusetts Infantry (MM 792)

Deery, John, and Augustus Morrison, 1st Louisiana Cavalry (LL 3253)

Doyle, John, 15th Maine Infantry (LL 1097)

Duncan, Henry, 4th USCT (MM 2547)

Enger, Frank, and Joseph Halroyed, 1st Louisiana Cavalry (OO 1017)

Ennis, Thomas, alias John W. Dodge, 6th Iowa Infantry (OO 945)

Geary, Daniel, and Ransom S. Gordon, 72nd New York Infantry (MM 1481)

Grippen, James, and Benjamin Redding, 104th USCT (MM 3184)

Hakes, George, 6th Michigan Cavalry (NN 3743)

Hall, John, 5th New Hampshire Infantry (MM 1909)

Halon, James, 20th New York Cavalry (LL 2552)

Hardin, Lewis, and Daniel Tierce, 13th USCT (NN 3232)

Helton, Charles, 39th Kentucky Mounted Infantry (NN 2919)

Hendricks, Abe, Confederate (MM 2900)

Herd, John F., citizen (NN 2140)

Herter, Anton, 17th Missouri Infantry (NN 3809)

Hill, Eden, 10th Missouri Infantry (MM 0660)

Hilton, William, 16th Indiana Infantry (LL 3201)

Holland, Perry, 1st Infantry Mississippi Marine Brigade (MM 1170)

Hooks, Thomas, Confederate (MM 3553)

Hughes, Robert Henry, quartermaster, alias William Johnson (MM 1470)

Hunter, Charles, 7th Kentucky Cavalry (NN 1921)

Jackson, William, 38th USCT (MM 1984)

John, Harvey, 49th Ohio Infantry (MM 742)

Johnson, James, Confederate (MM 1021)

Jones, William, 3rd Wisconsin Cavalry (NN 2113)

Kennedy, Richard, 56th New York Infantry (LL 2227)

Killgore, Thomas, and David Kunkle, 38th Ohio Infantry (MM 2471)

Lander, Anthony, 113th USCT Infantry (MM 3169)

Lauer, Charles F., 55th Pennsylvania Infantry (NN 624)

Lindsey, William, and Perry Pierson, 33rd Indiana Infantry (MM 746)

Magruder, Henry, Confederate (MM 2958)

Martin, John, and John Tully, 13th New York Cavalry (NN 2998)

McCarty, Arthur, 78th Ohio Infantry (MM 3937)

Mitchell, Thomas, 1st New York Engineers (OO 886)

Murphy, Henry, 35th Indiana Infantry (LL 298)

Nailin, Dow, and George Narin, citizens (MM 2571)

Nelson, George, 13th USCT (NN 2168)

Newton, William, 5th Vermont Infantry (NN 3066)

Nichols, John, Confederate (MM 746)

O'Malley, George, 115th Pennsylvania Infantry (MM 402)

Preble, James, 12th New York Cavalry (MM 1774 and OO 3428)

Ralph, Horace, 3rd Wisconsin Cavalry (LL 3132)

Rausher, Peter, 5th Pennsylvania Cavalry (OO 175)

Roberts, John S., 22nd Indiana Infantry (LL 2041)

Scott, Henry, 9th Kansas Cavalry (NN 3857)

Shehan, Michael, 8th Maine Infantry (OO 1320)

Sheppard, John, 38th USCT (MM 2006)

Smith, Andrew, 11th Pennsylvania Cavalry (NN 2099)

Sorg, Lewis, Jerry Spades, and Lewis Troest, 1st New York Artillery (KK 207)

Sperry, Charles, 13th New York Cavalry (NN 2427)

Stratchen, William (W.R.), Provost Marshal (NN 2169)

Swift, William, 72nd Indiana Infantry (LL 380)

Tully, Patrick, 12th New York Cavalry (NN 375)

Turchin, John B., 19th Illinois Infantry (KK 122)

Vincent, John, 3rd U.S. Cavalry (MM 3032)

Wallenus, Francois, Independent Battalion, New York Infantry (MM 1054)

Warner, A.C., 9th Illinois Mounted Infantry (MM 3937)

Wenz, Charles, 4th USCT Cavalry (MM 2780 and MM 3318)

Williams, Evan, 48th USCT (OO 1416)

Wilson, Benjamin, citizen teamster (II 999)

Confederate Court-Martial

Court martial file cited is located in Record Group 109, Confederate Adjutant and Inspector General Records, Chapter 1, Volume 3, in the National Archives and Records Administration, Washington, D.C.

Duncan, John, 3rd Tennessee

Microfilm

Microfilm records cited are located in the National Archives and Records Administration, Washington, D.C. After the name and unit of the defendant(s), the proceeding index number and location are provided in parentheses.

Baker, Wallace, John Cork, Spencer Lloyd, and John M. Smith, 55th Massachusetts Infantry (M1801, 78/02)

Blatner, Jacob, and John Williams, 4th West Virginia Cavalry (M508, 77/01)

Bravard, Dudley O., and John Linville, 54th Kentucky Infantry (M397, 75/06)

Brewer, Thomas H., 2nd Tennessee Mounted Infantry (M395, 75/10)

Catlett, Alfred, Alexander Colwell, Washington Jackson, and Charles Turner, 1st USCT Artillery (M1818, 77/04).

Deery, James, and Augustine Morrison, 1st Louisiana Cavalry (M396, 75/10)

Enger, Francis, and Joseph Holroyed, 1st Louisiana Cavalry (M396, 75/10)

Farmer, William B., 1st Arkansas Cavalry (M399, 75/04)

Hardin, Lewis, George Nelson, and Daniel Tierce, 13th USCT Infantry (M1821, 77/10)

Helton, Charles, 39th Kentucky Infantry (M397, 75/06)

Hill, Eden C., 10th Missouri Infantry (M405, 76/02)

Hunter, Charles, 7th Kentucky Cavalry (M397, 75/06)

Kemp, Lawson, 55th USCT Infantry (M2000, 78/02)

Kimball, Charles O., 2nd Arkansas Infantry (M399, 75/04)

Mitchell, Thomas, 1st New York Engineer (M2004, 79/01)

Wenz, Charles, 4th USCT Cavalry (M1817, 77/03)

Williams, Evan, 48th USCT Infantry (M2000, 78/02)

Compiled Military Service Records (CMSR)

Compiled Military Service Records (CMSR) cited are located in the National Archives and Records Administration, Washington, D.C.

Allison, Calvin Asbury, Wisner Condra, Henry Lowery, John Buckhanan Mills, Adam Patrick Scott, and Gaines Simco, 14th Kansas Cavalry

Atwell, Robert H., 2nd Kansas Cavalry

Bell, John, 2nd Kansas Cavalry

Bond, Thomas, 9th Pennsylvania Reserve Infantry

Bork, Adolph, 183rd Ohio Infantry

Callaghan, John, Thomas Johnson, and Jacob Snover, 2nd New Jersey Cavalry

Carrol, John, 20th Wisconsin Cavalry

Childers, Joshua, George R. Hoopengarner, Lewis Sappington, and Mark Tulley, 52nd Indiana Infantry

Chinock, William C., 26th Massachusetts Infantry

Christian, Robert, 5th New York Cavalry

Clark, Charles, 20th New York Cavalry

Curham, James H., 1st New York Mounted Rifles

Dawson, Thomas R., 19th Massachusetts Infantry

Ennis, Thomas, alias John W. Dodge, 6th Iowa Infantry

Geary, Daniel, and Ransom Gordon, 72nd New York Infantry

Hakes, George, 6th Michigan Cavalry

Hilton, William, 16th Indiana Mounted Infantry

Holland, Perry, 1st Mississippi Marine Brigade Infantry

Jay, Henry, 57th USCT Infantry

John, Harvey, 49th Ohio Infantry

Jones, William, and Horace Ralph, 3rd Wisconsin Cavalry

Killgore, Thomas, and David Kunkle, 38th Ohio Infantry

Murphy, Henry, 35th Indiana Infantry

O'Malley, George, 115th Pennsylvania Infantry

Pierson, Perry, 33rd Indiana Infantry

Preble, James, 12th New York Cavalry

Redmond, Joseph, 20th New York Cavalry

Rucker, Edward, 6th Kansas Cavalry

Shean, Michael, 8th Maine Infantry

Sorg, Louis, and Lewis Trost, 1st New York Artillery

Sperry, Charles, 13th New York Cavalry

Tully, Patrick, 12th New York Cavalry

Vincent, John, 11th New Hampshire Infantry

Newspaper and Periodical Collections

Agitator (PA)

Altoona Tribune (PA)

American Citizen (Canton, MS)
American Missionary
Arkansas True Democrat
Austin State Gazette
Charleston Mercury
Chicago Tribune
Christian Recorder (PA)
Daily Evening Bulletin (PA)
Daily Times (Leavenworth, KS)
Erie Observer (PA)
Galveston Weekly News
Harper's Weekly
Liberty Weekly Tribune (MO)
Louisville Daily Journal
Macon Telegraph (GA)
Memphis Daily Appeal
Missouri Democrat
Nashville Daily Union
Newark Advocate (OH)
New York Herald
New York Times
North American and United States Gazette (PA)
Press (PA)
Raleigh Register
Republican Compiler (PA)
Richmond Daily Dispatch
Richmond Examiner
Richmond Whig
Rolla Express (MO)
San Antonio Herald
Savannah Republican
Staunton Spectator (VA)
Tuscaloosa Observer (AL)

Court Cases

Blackburn v. State. 22 Ohio St. 102 (1871).
Camp v. State. 3 Ga. 417 (1847).

Cato v. State. 9 Fla. 163 (1860).

Commonwealth v. Fields. 31 Va. 648 (1832).

Commonwealth v. Thomas. 3 Va. 307 (1812).

Croghan v. State. 22 Wis. 444 (1868).

George v. State. 37 Miss. 316 (1859).

Grandison v. State. 21 Tenn. 451 (1841).

People v. Abbot. 19 Wend. (N.Y.) 192 (1838).

People v. Benson. 6 Cal. 221 (1856).

People v. Hulse. 3 Hill (N.Y.) 309 (1842).

Pleasant v. State. 13 Ark. 360 (1853).

Pollard v. State. 2 Iowa 567 (1856).

State v. Bender. 1 Del. Cas. 278 (1793).

State v. Blake. 39 Me. 322 (1855).

State v. Gray. 53 N.C. 170 (1860).

State v. Hartigan. 32 Vt. 607 (1860).

State v. Jim. 48 N.C. 348 (1856).

State v. Peter. 53 N.C. 19 (1860).

State v. Peter. 14 La. Ann. 521 (1859).

State v. Sam. 60 N.C. 300 (1864).

State v. Tomlinson. 11 Iowa 401 (1861).

Stephen v. State. 11 Ga. 225 (1852).

United States v. Patrick. 27 F. Cas. (District of Columbia) 460 (1812).

Index

Made in the USA
Lexington, KY
03 September 2016